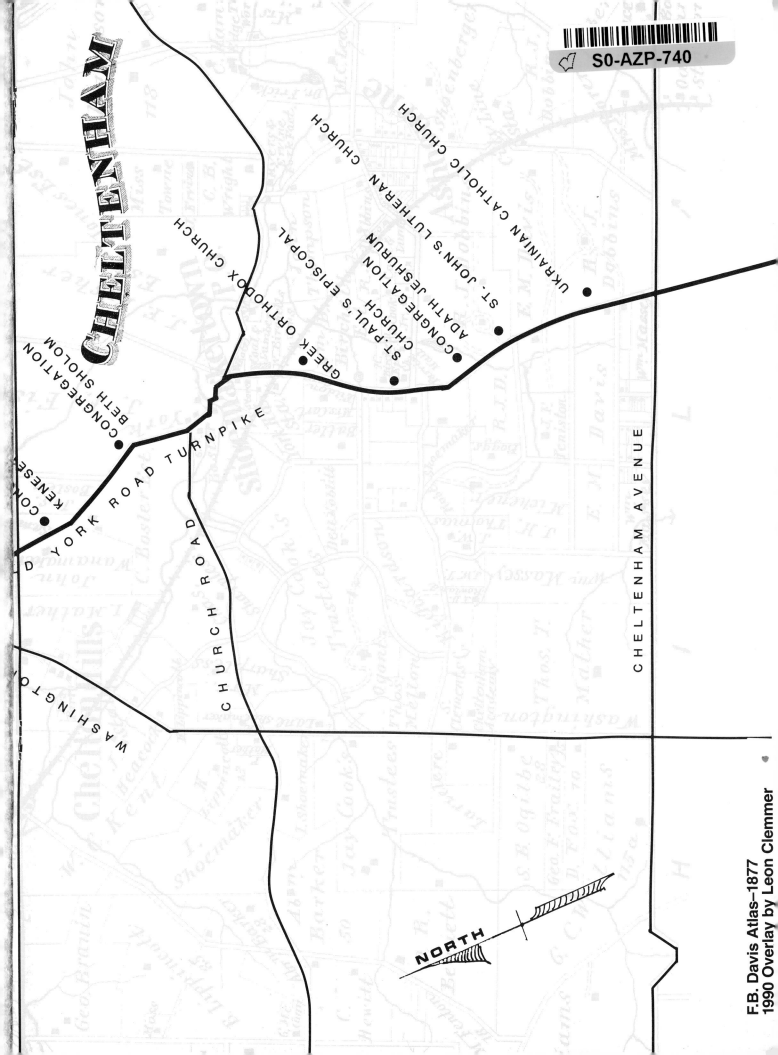

CHELTENHAM

F.B. Davis Atlas–1877
1990 Overlay by Leon Clemmer

S0-AZP-740

8/14/92

To Seth,

Mazal Tov on your graduation and your new job. I will truly miss you once you have left. Hope this helps remind you of your years at KRC.

Love,
Reena, Jeremy
Ari + Elana

One God
SIXTEEN HOUSES

by **Simeon J. Maslin**

with Phyllis Agins Grode and Leon Clemmer

Photography: Michael McGuire and George Salkin

An Illustrated Introduction to the Churches and Synagogues
of the Old York Road Corridor

"Come, let us go up to the house of God."
— Isaiah 2:3

To Our Grandchildren

Kathy   Jonathan

   Marianne   Amiel

     Joanna   Benjamin

              Yair

                Tamar

and to yours.

May their generation see that promised day when
"They shall not hurt or destroy
in all My holy mountain;
for the earth shall be full
of the knowledge of God
as the waters cover the sea."

Production Manager   James Gibson
Layout/Composition   Maureen Hardwick
Cover and Text Design   David Saltzberg
Printed by   Waldman Graphics

Printed in the United States of America

Maslin, Simeon J.
    One God, Sixteen Houses; An Illustrated Introduction to the Churches and Synagogues of the Old York Road Corridor; by Simeon J. Maslin with Phyllis Agins Grode and Leon Clemmer. Elkins Park, PA: Reform Congregation Keneseth Israel, c.1990.
    200 p: maps

1. Church architecture-PA-history. 2. Synagogue architecture-PA-history. 3. Synagogues-PA-history. 4. Churches-PA-history. 5. Congregations-PA-history. I. Clemmer, Leon. II. Grode, Phyllis Agins. III. Title
974.8 Mas
ISBN 0-9627062-0-5

Table of Contents

Foreword

This book was inspired by the spirit of collegiality and mutual respect that prevails whenever the members of the Jenkintown Ministerium meet. Occasionally, those meetings are for business, i.e. to plan the annual community Thanksgiving and Baccalaureate services and the ecumenical Christian Good Friday service or to listen to a guest scholar, but more often the meetings simply provide an opportunity to share a lunch and to get to know one another better.

As the idea for this book began to evolve, I shared it with my colleagues who were very encouraging. I then discussed it with a dear friend and member of my own congregation, Janice Bers, who has a long record of involvement in the charitable institutions of Abington, Jenkintown and Cheltenham. She too liked the idea and shared it with her philanthropist husband, Julian. To my delight Janice and Julian decided to sponsor the publication of this book as a gift of love to the churches and synagogues of their community. And so primary thanks for the encouragement and wherewithal to undertake this project goes to my colleagues and to Janice and Julian Bers.

After a couple of years of attempting to find an hour here and there to gather and edit the material for this book, I came to the realization that it needed a researcher with a gift for writing. I found the ideal person on the faculty of our Keneseth Israel Religious School — Phyllis Agins Grode, a talented emerging author, a friend and a much needed prodder.

Most of the material in the sixteen "History" and "Tour" sections was written by Ms. Grode herself; some was prepared by clergy or by volunteers from the several congregations. Whenever the major source of information was a volunteer, that person is so identified. We thank all of those church and synagogue members who thus offered their time for the benefit of their congregations.

A very valuable source for historical and architectural information, and later another much needed prodder, was Leon Clemmer. Not only did Mr. Clemmer write the introductory historical essay, "Old York Road: A Trail of American History," and prepare the end-paper map, but he served as a valuable source of information and a willing and friendly consultant. Heart-felt gratitude to my collaborators, Phyllis Agins Grode and Leon Clemmer.

Photography is a major part of this book, and the original photographic work was done by Mr. George Salkin of New York. In the later stages of editing, it became clear that many more pictures would be needed to do even partial justice to these unique houses of worship. It was then that we found a talented and imaginative local photographer, Michael McGuire of Jenkintown, who is the source of most of the black and white and some of the color photographs. Sincere thanks to Mr. Salkin and to Mr. McGuire for their talent and for sharing our joy in this labor.

Thanks also to my devoted secretary, Marilyn Baltz, for the many hours of meticulous and painstaking labor that she devoted to this volume. And thanks to Vivian Dow and Nina Salkin for their good counsel when the idea for this book was germinating. A word of gratitude also to Mr. Charles Harrison for his wise counsel about printing and publication.

Above all, thanks to God, the ultimate source of this and every worthy endeavor. May the loving praise of generations yet unborn ascend from our sixteen houses to the Abode of Glory. Amen.

Simeon J. Maslin
Congregation Keneseth Israel
June 1, 1990

Heroes, Benefactors and Preachers in Stained Glass

George Whitefield, Malachi Jones, Benjamin Harrison, John Wanamaker and William Jennings Bryan *Evangelist, First Pastor, U.S. President, Merchant, Orator — all part of the history of this church.*

— The Chapel
Abington Presbyterian Church

Robert Morris and Haym Salomon *Philadelphia patriots and Revolutionary War financiers, shown before Independence Hall, with the Liberty Bell.*

— Neumann Chapel
Congregation Keneseth Israel

John Wanamaker *Merchant and Founder of Grace Presbyterian, shown before City Hall, Wanamaker's, and the Church.*

— Wanamaker Chapel
Grace Presbyterian Church

Martin Luther King, Jr. *Martyred hero of civil rights, preacher at Salem and friend of the Pastor.*

— Rev. M. L. King, Jr., Chapel
Salem Baptist Church

Introduction

There may be considerable theological, ethnic and ritual distance between Ukrainian Catholics and Presbyterians, but on Old York Road less than four miles separate the Church of the Annunciation of the Blessed Virgin Mary and Abington Presbyterian Church. And between them, along that brief stretch of road winding through Melrose Park, Elkins Park, Jenkintown and Abington, are nine other sanctuaries dedicated to the glory of God. Add a little loop off the main road in Jenkintown, and you pass five more — a total of sixteen historic and beautiful houses of worship representing virtually the entire Judeo-Christian tradition of America. Thus our title: *One God, Sixteen Houses.*

Crossing Cheltenham Avenue from Philadelphia into the northern suburbs via Old York Road, the three golden, onion-top steeples of the Ukrainian Catholic Church of the Annunciation come immediately into view. Using that first church as our starting point, we find the following, all on the *right* side of the road:

Mileage

0.0 Church of the Annunciation of the Blessed Virgin Mary (Ukrainian Catholic Church)

0.3 St. John's Evangelical Lutheran Church

0.6 Congregation Adath Jeshurun (Jewish Conservative)

0.7 St. Paul's Episcopal Church

0.9 Church of the Annunciation (Greek Orthodox)

1.6 Congregation Beth Sholom (Jewish Conservative)

1.9 Congregation Keneseth Israel (Jewish Reform)

2.6 Church of Our Saviour (Episcopalian)

2.7 Grace Presbyterian Church

3.5 Old York Road Temple Beth Am (Jewish Reform) and then, on the *left* side of the road,

3.8 Abington Presbyterian Church

This book concerns the churches and synagogues of the Old York Road corridor. But it was inspired by the good will and fellowship of the members of the Jenkintown Ministerium, and five of the churches represented in the Ministerium are located in a cluster just *off* Old York Road near the center of Jenkintown. To the *east* of our main thoroughfare are:

First Church of Christ, Scientist (West Avenue and Washington Lane)

Abington Friends Meeting (Meetinghouse Road and Greenwood Avenue)

And to the *west* are:

Immaculate Conception Church (Roman Catholic; 604 West Avenue)

Jenkintown United Methodist Church (328 Summit Avenue)

Salem Baptist Church (Summit Avenue and Leedom Street)

These, then, are the sixteen houses of worship covered in this volume. Several are typical English country churches; two evoke the exotic east; one is a striking example of architectural boldness; two have roots in mid-nineteenth-century Philadelphia; one predates the independence of the United States by a wide margin; and a remarkable seven are products of the demographic trends that brought large numbers of Philadelphia Christians to the northern suburbs along with the railroads in the nineteenth century.

One would be hard-pressed to find a comparable group of distinguished and historic churches along a four-mile stretch of roadway anywhere else in the United States. Most of the major American religious bodies are represented, while Episcopalians, Presbyterians, Conservative Jews, Reform Jews and Catholics are doubly represented. And, while the standard of living among the members of these sixteen congregations might be considerably higher than the national average, one cannot help but feel that there is something "typically American" about the Old York Road religious cluster.

Interestingly, there are no "fringe" religious groups among the sixteen. These are all well-established, mainstream churches and synagogues. This affluent suburban area must have its share of Pentecostals and charismatics, but somehow they have not situated themselves on Old York Road. Of interest also is the fact that such well-established denominations as the Latter-Day Saints (Mormons), United Church of Christ and Orthodox Jews are absent from the Old York Road cluster although present elsewhere in the area.

The purpose of this volume is to acquaint the people of Melrose Park, Elkins Park, Jenkintown, Abington and environs with the churches and synagogues to which they do *not* belong. People seem to be uncomfortable, possibly even frightened, at the idea of dropping in for a visit to a religious institution of another tradition. But there is so much commonality among the members of these several churches and synagogues. Most of them are middle-class business people and professionals. They adhere to the center of the American political spectrum. They tend to be not only civil but, when moved, charitable. They share values and aspirations. Yet ...

Yet they are reluctant to cross each others' religious thresholds. The "other" is strange, exotic, possibly even alien. But there is so much to be learned by opening oneself to the other. Every one of these sixteen distinguished houses of worship welcomes strangers — not for evangelistic purposes, not to "save" or convert, but quite simply to extend the hand of brotherhood and sisterhood.

During the past several years, the editor of this book has been invited to preach, to teach classes and to engage in dialogue in several area churches. One of the questions that he is asked most frequently is: "Are non-Jews allowed to attend services at your synagogue?" His answer — a question: "Are Jews allowed to attend services at your church?" Obviously the answer is Yes. And that is the answer — and the invitation — extended by the members and clergy of each of the sixteen churches and synagogues.

> "Have we not all one Mother/Father?
> Has not one God created us?"
> (*Malachi 2:10*)

We come from different religious traditions. We may even have diametrically opposed answers to some very basic questions. But we are neighbors, and we are all, in our sixteen separate "houses," children of the one God. As we come to know each other better — yes, even knowing how we *differ* — we add strength to our community and to the beloved United States of America where each man and woman is free to worship God according to the dictates of conscience.

Please consider this book to be your invitation to visit your neighbor's church or synagogue.

> *Peace*
> *Eirene*
> *Myr*
> *Pax*
> *Shalom*

> — Simeon J. Maslin

Old York Road: A Trail of American History

BY LEON CLEMMER

York Road is a trail of history where Indians once roamed and armies once marched. It is a microcosm of the growth of America. From the border of Philadelphia to Susquehanna Road, a distance of four miles, history is alive. It runs through an area where some of America's greatest wealth was lavished on huge estates and great art collections, where American and British troops skirmished during the Revolution, where the "underground railroad" had a station to receive fugitive slaves, and where thirty thousand black Union troops trained to fight under white officers during the Civil War.

York Road and the families who settled around it remind us of the "robber barons," of a world of intrigue and land speculation. Here houses of worship were built by people of great wealth, by great men and women of lesser means, by migrating ethno-religious communities, and one as the result of a railroad accident. All of these factors contributed to the growth of a vibrant community around the York Road corridor. But it was the arrival of the railroad that ultimately caused the greatest expansion and the growth of the whole area.

This book is the story of the sixteen churches that serve the Old York Road corridor and its immediate neighborhoods, sixteen congregations going back three centuries to the founding of the Abington Meeting of Friends. It is a story of individualists, of communities of belief, and of people of a wide variety of faiths and ethnic backgrounds.

A quick ride up York Road will reveal some interesting similarities and differences among the sixteen houses of worship. The York Road churches and synagogues — the eleven actually on York Road — are all, except for one, on the east side of the road. (The one on the west side, Abington Presbyterian, was also originally on the east side.) All are of masonry construction. No two were designed by the same architect. They vary in style from Frank Furness' solid Romanesque Church of Our Saviour to Frank Lloyd Wright's Beth Sholom. Only two congregations have moved, the Jenkintown Baptist and the Orthodox Friends, and only the Baptist Church has been torn down. The Immaculate Conception Catholic Church and Abington Presbyterian Church both burned down, but both were rebuilt on the same sites. York Road has seen great preachers and evangelists come and go through the years: Dwight Moody, Billy Sunday, Billy Graham, Martin Luther King, and, the earliest of all, George Whitefield in 1740. For the most part, the resident ministers, priests and rabbis have been able spokesmen for the mainstreams of their denominations, not flamboyant but faithful pastors to their congregations.

The York Road corridor is a classic example of development encouraged by ease of transportation and the siren song of the land speculator. The earliest history of the area is entwined with William Penn and the land speculators to whom he sold or gave pieces of his grant from the King of England. As early as 1683, we read of the "Proprietors," the grants, and absentee land owners. The now familiar names appear on the earliest maps of his surveyor, Thomas Holmes — Shoemaker, Wall and Leach in Cheltenham, Barnes and Holmes in what is now Abington.

But land that is inaccessible is worthless. In 1681 Thomas Holmes was commissioned to plot an overland route from the docks at the foot of Vine Street in Philadelphia to a terminus above what is now New Hope in Pennsylvania. It would be extended to an overland connection to the new "York," across New Jersey to the Hudson River.

Holmes also planned a road connecting the Dela-

Map of William Penn's Land Grants.

ware River to the Susquehanna. This road, now called Susquehanna Street Road, would intersect York Road on the hill beyond Cheltenham. Here the Moores would build an inn and tavern and the Presbyterians would build a small log church in 1714 on the east side of the York Road. The area would be called Mooretown, after the Moore's Tavern and Inn. Only later would it be called Abington. About a mile closer to Philadelphia, the Jenkins also built an inn on their 422 acres. This inn became a favorite stop for the stage coach, and the area soon became known as Jenkins' town or Jenkintown.

The Governor's Council authorized the first section of roadway to be built in 1693. The "York Road Turnpike," as it was named, was a private toll road. In 1711 the road was ordered extended to Bucks County. The Cheltenham and Willow Grove Turnpike Company built the first eleven miles from Philadelphia to Willow Grove at a cost of $8,000 per mile. Stone from the local quarries in the area, particularly Shoemakertown and Edge Hill, was used for the road bed. And so, with the dawn of the eighteenth century, ease of transportation and cheap land contributed to the rapid development of the area around York Road.

The initial settlers of the area around York Road were English. They came to the area, because it was in the hills and valleys north of Philadelphia that they found economic opportunity and the freedom to worship as they chose. The Quakers came first and worshipped in Cheltenham. Then in 1697, after John Barnes gave them 120 acres, they built their meeting house and burial ground just east of York Road in Abington. Their earliest burial ground remains, almost hidden, on Ashbourne Road, just west of York Road, in Cheltenham.

The Scotch-Irish built a log Presbyterian Church in Mooretown in 1714 on their ninety-four acres of land on the east side of the York road. This was the first home of Abington Presbyterian Church, as we know it today. The Episcopalians had already built St. Thomas in Whitemarsh in 1710. They shared a priest with Trinity Church in Oxford, and the path connecting the two churches became known as "the Church road."

Church Road crossed York Road at the site of a flowing creek, the Tookany. The creek meant water power, and water power meant the possibility of industrial development. It was at this intersection that Richard Wall built his house, which still stands today, and his mill. The area around it was called Shoemaker Town, after one of the early land grantees.

For the most part, this area north of Philadelphia was rolling attractive farmland, with a few mills, a couple of quarries, and a lot of forest between the houses and farms. The unspoiled nature of the area was attested to by Laura Barney, Jay Cooke's daughter, who described Indians still in the area as late as the 1850s.

Philadelphia, by contrast, had miserable summers, with high humidity, high temperatures and dense housing. In 1790, when the city was the capital of the new republic, the legislators recognized that the city was not a fit place to live in the summer, and so the capital was moved seasonally to Germantown. Those who could afford it maintained summer houses away from the city. The Chelten Hills were a favored location, as were the banks of the Delaware, Schuylkill and the Wissahickon.

During the American Revolution, it was York Road, not Washington Lane, that was the route of the armies, both American and British. They marched to Trenton and back again along York Road, and they skirmished in the hills along the York Road corridor. The four Colonial soldiers buried in the Abington Presbyterian Church graveyard at the southeast corner of York and Susquehanna bear silent witness to the activity of the armies in the area.

The York Road corridor served a peaceful and stable religious community during the years between the Revolutionary and the Civil Wars. There was a minor disruption when, in 1830, a Meeting House was built in Jenkintown, the result of the split in the Quaker community between the Orthodox and Hicksite factions. The Orthodox group built their little Meeting House on Jenkintown Road, and that building still stands today in Alverthorpe Park, the only church building in the community to be abandoned. The Lyceum, in Jenkintown, built in 1832 served as the first home of several churches and serves today as the Jenkintown Public Library. The Abington Library Society bought the Jenkintown Lyceum Building from the Lyceum Society in 1909 for $10,000. In 1976 the name was changed from the Abington to the Jenkintown Library.

The area remained a quiet bedroom community and farming area through the first half of the nineteenth century. The first of the "big names" to establish residence in the York Road corridor was Jay Cooke who summered near what is today Ashbourne Road and Penrose Avenue. But then, with the coming of the railroad to Chelten Hills in 1854, the bucolic serenity of the area began to change dramatically.

The connection between Philadelphia and the anthracite coal mines near Bethlehem and Reading ran through Jenkintown. First in 1855 came the North Pennsylvania Railroad, later shortened to the North Penn. It was to run diagonally across the state from Philadelphia to Bradford County, to connect with the Erie Railroad. The road went bankrupt and was taken over in 1879 by the Philadelphia and Reading Railroad Company, headed by J.P. Morgan. Earlier the connections had been made for service to New Hope in 1872 and to New York in 1876.

The last stagecoach run was in 1872. The jolting ride from Philadelphia to Doylestown cost seventy-five cents, one way, and took fifteen hours in 1815. But Jenkintown changed from a stagecoach stop to the hub of the rail transportation system in the 1870s. By 1897 seventy-four passenger trains passed through the area each day. The fare in 1900 was ten cents for the twenty-one minute ride from Jenkintown to

Jay Cooke/Lucretia Mott

midcity Philadelphia's new Reading Terminal. By comparison, the carriage trip to Philadelphia was measured in hours.

Jay Cooke was the major financier of the Union during the Civil War, but another York Road area resident, Lucretia Mott, was one of the great preachers of the abolitionist movement that sparked the war. Quaker, abolitionist, preacher and feminist, Lucretia Mott gained national notoriety. Her home, "Roadside," located on York Road where the gates to Latham Park now stand, was the local station of the underground railroad. The fiery abolitionist preached, wrote and, in the days when Camp William Penn trained black troops on the property of her son-in-law Edward M. Davis behind her house, she ministered to the troops. John Brown's wife was a guest at "Roadside" when the Federal troops, under command of Robert E. Lee, captured and hanged Brown.

Lucretia Mott was probably the most influential woman in the movement to secure freedom for Blacks and equal rights for women throughout the nation until her death in 1883. Following the war, son-in-law Edward Davis became one of the area's earliest land developers. His first project was the selling of his land, which had been used for Camp William Penn, and then selling the wood from the buildings for the construction of "Camptown," later to be known as LaMott in memory of his mother-in-law.

By mid-nineteenth century Philadelphia "old money" still lived in center city, most of it in residences around Rittenhouse Square, while the "Main Line," on the west bank of the Schuylkill, had become the socially acceptable suburb. The Civil War changed that pattern. New wealth came with the war, and social patterns changed.

The first expansion of the church population along York Road began just before the war, as a direct result of the expansion of the railroad. Presbyterians and Methodists first gathered to worship in the Lyceum in Jenkintown in 1845. Then came the Catholics in 1850 and the Episcopalians in 1855. All four groups began their York Road area history in the Lyceum.

Real growth, however, came with the end of the Civil War. The new great wealth moved to the Chelten Hills. Financier Jay Cooke started to construct "Ogontz," his fifty-four room, one-and-a-half million dollar home, just as Richmond fell to the Union troops. His stated purpose was "to give employment to the returning veterans." Merchant, and later Postmaster, John Wanamaker, moved to Cheltenham in 1868 and started construction of his great mansion "Lindenhurst" on York Road in 1883. He even built his own train station, "Chelten Hills" (also known as "Ogontz").

Both Cooke and Wanamaker were deeply religious men. Cooke worshipped as an Episcopalian at Third and Walnut Streets in Philadelphia; Wanamaker, a Presbyterian, worshipped at Twenty-first and Walnut. Both summered in the Chelten Hills. Cooke grew tired of traveling back and forth to the City every Sunday after he moved to Cheltenham. It was Cooke's custom to return to his city church every Sunday morning for worship, followed by lunch, Bible study and then afternoon services. He would then return to his suburban home and meet with neighbors to conduct a men's Bible study class.

Cooke's daughter, Laura Barney, explained that the trip to town was an alternative to an equally arduous trip to Chestnut Hill or to Oxford. Interestingly, she ignored the mention of the nearby Church of Our Saviour in Jenkintown which had been founded in 1855. Since Cooke had already started a Bible study class in his home, it was only logical that he would proceed to establish his own Episcopalian church. He, along with his brother-in-law, William G. Morehead, his friends, George and John W. Thomas and a few others, continued to meet in homes for several years. But then he bought a parcel of land, and the group built their own church in 1861. That church was St. Paul's Episcopal at the intersection of Ashbourne Road and York Road.

Laura Barney wrote about the dedication of the church; she described the dogs' tails beating in time to the organ music under the benches, while the flies and mosquitos formed halos about the flames of the candles. Mr. Cooke and Mr. Thomas greeted the

Jenkintown Lyceum (now Public Library)

Chelten Hills Station (also known as Ogontz Station; now home of model railroad)

John Wanamaker's "Lindenhurst"

parishioners at the door and presided over the collection. Early church records bear witness to considerable activity on behalf of the Union troops during the war. There was the ministry of the church ladies to the black soldiers at Camp William Penn (LaMott), and aid to the troops at the battlefields of Gettysburg and Antietam.

Wanamaker, a Presbyterian, first attended the Abington Presbyterian Church after moving to Cheltenham, but then he switched to a joint affiliation with Grace Presbyterian in Jenkintown and the older Abington Church. Wanamaker provided the new bell to replace the one that melted in the great fire that destroyed the Abington Church building in 1895. He also hosted President Benjamin Harrison when he attended services in the church. Wanamaker had a great love for Sunday schools. When he joined the young Grace Presbyterian Church, he financed their first building, the Sunday School, and he personally led the new worshipers across the street from the Lyceum, where they had been meeting, into the new structure.

In the aftermath of the Civil War, the York Road area became a veritable mecca for new wealth. The pattern was repeated again and again. First, a summer house, then the mansion. With the mansions came the servants, the stables, the greenhouses and the farms. Workers to maintain these huge properties were imported and housed nearby. And in the footsteps of the great financiers and merchants came the near-great and the service businesses that these estates and their masters required.

William Lukens Elkins and Peter Arrell Brown Widener were partners in traction, oil, utilities (both gas and electric), gasoline refineries and, with other partners, organized U.S. Steel, American Tobacco and other major corporations. They served on the board of the Pennsylvania Railroad, and at the time of his death in 1903, Elkins was on the boards of one hundred corporations.

Elkins and Widener must be counted among the great entrepreneurs of post-Civil War America. Both were born in the 1830s; both, instead of serving in the war, went to work in retail establishments; both established themselves in food businesses first, Widener as a butcher, Elkins as a produce distributor, and then branched out into other businesses. Widener expanded into horse traction lines and meat stores; Elkins went into oil in western Pennsylvania. Widener served for a short time as the Treasurer of Philadelphia.

Both men, after making huge fortunes, built large mansions on North Broad Street, far from the social center of Rittenhouse Square, and then, in 1890, they both built magnificent Trumbauer-designed mansions in Chelten Hills. Elkins named his Italian Renaissance residence Elstowe Park, and Widener

P.A.B. Widener/William L. Elkins

named his nearby Versailles-scale palace Lynnewood Hall. They lived in a manner unmatched in Philadelphia, and, in fact, in most of America. Yet, despite the opulence of their Chelten Hills mansions, both spent their summers in Newport, Rhode Island, and the "seasons" in Philadelphia and New York.

Widener gave a major part of his fortune to the City of Philadelphia by way of the Widener Home for Crippled Children in Olney. His art collection ultimately was given to the nation and may be viewed today in the National Gallery of Art in Washington, D.C. The Elkins were especially generous to the Masonic Home and to Abington Hospital. Their art collection was given to the City of Philadelphia and can be seen in the Philadelphia Museum of Art. Widener's son, George, was Chairman of the Cheltenham Township Commissioners at the time of his death on the unsinkable *Titanic* in 1912. Elkin's son, George, founded Abington Hospital.

Today we can see only the shells of some of the great buildings and outbuildings of these huge estates. It is difficult to comprehend the staffs — gardeners, farmers, horsemen, grooms, butlers and maids — that were required to maintain them. Each was almost self-sufficient, with farms, greenhouses and stables. Widener actually went one step further with a full race track, steeplechase and public races. It was often

said of the Chelten Hills area in the waning years of the nineteenth century that there were "more millionaires per acre than in any other part of the country."

In addition to their huge personal estates, these millionaire entrepreneurs controlled hundreds of acres of land around Old York Road that was ripe for

P.A.B. Widener's "Lynnewood Hall"

development. Widener, Elkins, Wanamaker, Newbold, Curtis, Roberts, Lippincott and Asbury all owned large tracts of land, and many smaller developers joined in the great rush of land speculation. William T. B. Roberts, who built the great mansions for Elkins and Widener, built three thousand homes in the area. He wrote in an 1897 promotional piece that "with the addition of many beautiful and artistic homes, Ogontz Park (today's Elkins Park) represents all that is possible in the making of a high class, exclusive residential suburb."

Major land owners like Elkins, Widener and Wanamaker, with their agents, became the promoters and developers of vast areas of York Road and Easton Road. Wanamaker owned large parts of Wyncote, Baederwood, Rydal and Meadowbrook. Elkins owned all of old Abington, and, with Roberts, owned Ogontz, Glenside, Ardsley, Roslyn and Willow Grove. Their developments brought to the area the people who filled the churches and constituted the society of the York Road area.

Along with their shrewd business ability, most of these men felt the need to give some of their money back to the community. They built "their" churches, or, in some cases, embellished those that were already there. Newbold built Jenkintown's Church of Our Saviour; Herbert and Miller built St. John's Lutheran Church on land given to them by Elkins; and Curtis paid off the mortgage at All Hallows Episcopal.

Widener expanded St. Pauls' three times between 1897 and 1923, the greatest of these expansions in memory of George and Harry Widener who perished on the *Titanic* in 1912. Elkins gave the organ to St. Pauls', and each gave some of the thirteen Louis Tiffany windows.

The freed slaves and returning black troops built their churches too, Salem Baptist in Jenkintown and the LaMott AME Church. LaMott is the area that was once Camptown, the site of Camp William Penn, the training camp for the black troops in the Civil War.

World War I slowed the growth of the area for a couple of years, but the roaring twenties brought more expansion and development. Once again, the new wealth following the war brought more residents. Three country clubs — Old York Road (1910), Huntingdon Valley (1898), and Philmont (1907) — created an elite social atmosphere for families considering the move from city to suburbs. The cry of the land speculator was heard again.

York Road had been privately owned by the Cheltenham and Willow Grove Turnpike Company since 1803. The toll was three cents for a horse and twenty cents for a coach. Around the turn of the century the toll charges were raised to one cent per bike, five cents per automobile and ten cents per truck. In 1884 Elkins and Widener added trolley tracks from Philadelphia to Doylestown. And then in 1895 Willow

York Road Toll House

Grove Park was opened to attract passengers. There were excursions in open trolley cars to hear John Philip Sousa and to see the great fireworks displays.

The trolley car and the street railroad provided more impetus to the expansion of the York Road corridor. For seven-and-one-half cents or a token, one could board a trolley at the Navy Yard in south Philadelphia and ride to Doylestown, Media or Chestnut Hill. One could even ship freight on a trolley; the Jenkintown freight station was on York Road across from Grace Presbyterian Church. The U.S. Mail had special trolley cars, and department stores also shipped purchases by the trolley. There were even funeral trolleys with the pall bearers and the family in a properly crepe-draped car and the casket in a compartment up front. During the first decades of the twentieth century, it was the Old York Road trolley that made the north suburban area so convenient. One could live in the beautiful country-side with easy access to the City.

As people moved north and the new housing developments were occupied, so too were the York Road area churches populated by many new parishioners. Already in existence in our suburban area before World War I were the Abington Meeting of Friends, Abington Presbyterian, Salem Baptist, Jenkintown United Methodist, Grace Presbyterian, Church of Our Saviour, Immaculate Conception, St. Paul's Episcopal and St. John's Lutheran — nine of

the sixteen houses of worship covered in this volume. Only one additional church was built between the two World Wars; the Church of Christ Scientist in Jenkintown was built in 1937-38. The four synagogues and the two ethnic churches were built after World War II.

World War I was followed by "the roaring twenties." The newspapers were full of guest lists of the parties and balls at the mansions of the Wideners, the Elkins, the Sinklers and the Curtis'. Then came the Depression years and income taxes, followed by World War II; these combined to put an end to the great estates. The land was sold, most of the huge mansions demolished, and the art collections were either given to the great museums or sold. A servant class was a thing of the past, and the social scene moved to Chestnut Hill.

The Elkins property has been owned since the mid 1930s by the Dominican Order and used as a retreat house. The Wideners' Lynnewood Hall is today's Faith Theological Seminary. Both are mere shadows of their former glory. What was the racetrack is now Lynnewood Gardens, the Philadelphia area's largest (more than 1700 units) apartment complex. Curtis Hall was demolished to save taxes; only the music room remains. The Wanamaker mansion burned. Cooke's, Barney's and Stetson's homes were all demolished and the land used for multiple houses and apartments in their stead.

Cooke's mansion survived for a while as the Ogontz School for Young Ladies. (Amelia Earhart, who attended classes there for a short period, was probably the school's most famous student.) Ultimately, it too would be torn down and replaced by Eleanor Widener Dixon's Trumbauer-designed "Rondell Manor," which in turn would also be demolished to make way for a housing development, "Homes of Elkins Park."

The period of greatest expansion and change in the Old York Road corridor followed World War II. The automobile was king. The street railroads were taken over by the transit authorities and ultimately replaced by buses. York Road had been bought by Widener after a conflict developed between his street railroad and the toll road, but that conflict was finally resolved when the State of Pennsylvania took over

"55 Trolley" to Willow Grove

the ownership of the road in 1918 for $80,000. The toll was abolished.

The railroad suffered from disuse, and it too was taken over by the Rail Authority. What remained of the large land holdings was subdivided into small lots and development continued.

In the decade leading up to World War II, there was a steady influx of Jewish families into the York Road corridor. There had been several Jewish merchants in the area since around the turn of the century, but only a few had actually settled there. For the most part the synagogues were in the old sections of the city, particularly along North Broad Street.

Jewish settlement in Philadelphia goes back to the Colonial period. Congregation Mikveh Israel, located today in new quarters on Independence Mall, was founded forty years before the Revolutionary War, around the same time as historic Episcopalian Christ Church. Several more synagogues were founded in the early decades of the nineteenth century. But the first Jewish congregation to actually locate in the York Road area was Temple Judea which dedicated its synagogue just south of the Cheltenham Township line in 1939.

Only one of the pre-World War II Jewish settlers approached the grand style of mansion building of the Wideners, Wanamakers and their generations, and that was Lessing J. Rosenwald. Rosenwald built his mansion, Alverthorpe, in 1938 on Meetinghouse Road in Abington. Rosenwald, who was chairman of the board of Sears Roebuck, was probably America's foremost collector of prints. He donated his estate and mansion to Abington township in the 1960s; his print and art collections were given to the National Gallery of Art upon his death in 1979.

Three of the North Broad Street synagogues — Reform Congregation Keneseth Israel (1847), Congregation Adath Jeshurun (1859) and Congregation Beth Sholom (1918) — followed the main body of their congregants to the north suburban area in the 1950s, and all built large synagogues on York Road in Cheltenham among the pre-existing churches. (A fourth congregation, Rodeph Shalom, 1795, remained in the city on North Broad Street but established a branch in Elkins Park, several blocks east of York Road.) The one synagogue in Abington, Old York Road Temple Beth Am, was founded as a new suburban congregation in 1947.

The two newest churches, the Greek Orthodox and the Ukrainian Catholic, are also located in Cheltenham. The former, Church of the Annunciation, followed the York Road pattern: first a wealthy

Lessing Rosenwald's "Alverthorpe"

patron, Constantine Stephano, built a small chapel next to his home. The congregation expanded and then, in 1972, an attractive, Byzantine-style church was consecrated on the site of the W.T.B. Roberts mansion. The Ukrainian Church of the Annunciation located in Cheltenham at the decision of the Archbishop in 1968.

What of the future? Old patterns persist. In 1988 a new congregation began worshipping in the old Lyceum in Jenkintown, The New Testament Baptist Church. For a short period the New Life Presbyterian Church met at the former Abington Friends School, but it has since moved to Glenside. And a new Korean congregation now worships at the Church of Our Saviour in Jenkintown.

Growth continues and, with it, change. The York Road corridor has grown from Mooretown and Jenkins' Inn to a truly cosmopolitan and mixed neighborhood. In its variety is its strength; in its diversity is its uniqueness. Truly, we all walk on different paths and go to various houses, but our common goal is to reach the One God.

Church of the Annunciation

Church of the Annunciation of the Blessed Virgin Mary
(Ukrainian Catholic Church)
Corner of Old York Road and Valley Road, Melrose Park

HISTORY*

The twenty-five year history of Annunciation B.V.M. Ukrainian Catholic Church in Melrose Park, Pennsylvania, is a history not of dates or buildings but a history of people, of the founders and parishioners and of the priests who served them.

It was Archbishop Ambrose Senyshyn, head of the Ukrainian Catholic Archdiocese of Philadelphia who, in the spring of 1962, began to seek a suitable property for the establishment of a parish in the suburbs of Philadelphia. The site, at 1206 Valley Road, was purchased in April. Ten days after settlement, Father Paul Burak was named its first pastor. Archbishop Senyshyn named the parish in honor of the Mother of God (Theotokos) with the title Annunciation of the Blessed Virgin Mary. The Antimension for the altar was signed by the Metropolitan on August 14, 1962. The first Sunday liturgy was celebrated on August 26, 1962 in one of the larger rooms of the new house which had been converted into a chapel. This day was the beginning of a new era for the Ukrainian Catholic church in Philadelphia.

Before 1962 came to an end, Father Burak had formed an Altar Boys Society, the League of Ukrainian Catholic Youth and a parish choir under the direction of its first cantor, Jaroslaw Shchuka. The parish soon attracted one hundred registered families. Additional land was purchased on Valley Road. The present rectory was added on August 23, 1963.

Archbishop Senyshyn made his first canonical visitation to the parish on February 16, 1964. On July 16, 1964, he instructed Father Burak to build a new church with a seating capacity of 400 to 500 people. The building plans for the church were finalized in 1968 when Ricker and Axt were hired as architects to design the church and P. Agnes, Inc. was chosen as

the contractor. Rev. Monsignor Myroslaw Charyna officiated at the ceremony and represented Archbishop Senyshyn. Services were held at Holy Trinity Ruthenian Catholic Church in East Oak Lane until the new church was completed. It was during that time that Professor John Onuskanish came out of retirement to serve as director and cantor of the parish choir.

Father Burak's failing health necessitated his transfer to a parish where lighter duties would enable him to recover. He was appointed pastor of St. John the Baptist Ukrainian Catholic Church in McKeesport, Pennsylvania where he served from 1970 until his death in 1987.

On March 9, 1970, Very Rev. Constantine Berdar was named pastor of the Annunciation parish and served until 1972. Bishop Stock made a canonical visitation to the parish on December 5, 1971.

Very Rev. Augustine Molodowitz was named administrator of the parish on April 21, 1972. He served as administrator until May 1 when Bishop Stock became the third pastor of Annunciation B.V.M. Church. Bishop Stock's tenure was brief; he was killed in a car accident on June 29, 1972.

Rev. Robert Moskal succeeded the late Bishop as pastor. An exciting event took place a year after he began to serve. The cornerstone was blessed not only by Archbishop Senyshyn but also by the prime hierarch of the Ukrainian Catholic Church, Major Archbishop Joseph Cardinal Slipij. The blessing took place on May 13, 1973.

Several priests have served Annunciation Parish. The late Very Rev. Nicholas Kohut, OSBM, Rev. Hilary Benedict, OSBM, Rev. Joseph Korban, CSSR, and Rev. Alex Burak, brother of the late Father Paul served during Father Burak's illness; Father Michael Batcho served as a deacon from March to May, 1973,

---

*We are grateful to Helen T. Chaykowsky for preparing this history.

prior to his ordination. Father Thomas Sayuk resided at the parish after his ordination. Other priests who assisted the pastors were Rev. Iwan Popil and Rev. Joseph Kisner.

Monsignor Michael Federowich was named pastor of Annunciation parish on September 1, 1974, and served until November, 1979. During Monsignor's pastorship, the adjoining property on N. 12th Street was purchased with the hope of establishing a diocesan catechetical center. Monsignor also arranged for church altars to be designed by Ukrainian artist, Christina Dochwat.

In November, 1979, Very Rev. Monsignor Basil Makuch took over as pastor and served the parish for less than two years. New altars were commissioned.

Rev. James Melnic, the present pastor, came to Annunciation on August 15, 1981 from St. Mary's Ukrainian Catholic Church in Solon, Ohio, where he was the founding pastor.

In the past nine years, under Father Melnic's stewardship, the parish has grown from 100 to over 400 families. Father reorganized the parish choir, and it is presently under the direction of Ihor Kusznir. In 1985, Father financed the taping of the choir's first professional record of Christmas music. Father commissioned Ukrainian iconographer Andrij Maday to do the new iconostasis and interior painting of the church. The work is in the final stages of completion. A mosaic for the exterior of the church was designed and installed by Christina Dochwat.

Under his pastorate a new bell and carillon system and new exterior church doors were installed. Other improvements to parish grounds and sacristy were also made. Father plans to do extensive repairs and renovations to the adjoining church property so that it can serve as a much needed parish catechetical center, meeting rooms and parish facility.

Father James Melnic established the catechetical program. The director of the program is Mrs. Halia Mazurok-Reh who has two lay catechists to assist. The Sister Servants Markiana and Thomas (Chancellor of the Archdiocese) complete the teaching staff. Each Sunday after liturgy, forty-one children attend religion classes.

The spiritual growth of Annunciation B.V.M. parish since its founding in 1962 is a tribute to its founding pastor, Father Paul Burak, Archbishop Ambrose Senyshyn, the priests and pastors who served it and continue to serve and to the sterling generosity of its parishioners. Having celebrated our Silver Jubilee in 1987, we look forward with vision and hope to a golden future.

"Peace to those who enter." Stained glass, icons and
light combine to make a place where men and women meet God.

Church of the Annunciation of the Blessed Virgin Mary

TOUR

Exterior mosaic above entrance to Church, depicting the Annunciation.

Three gold leaf cupolas or *Banya* adorn the roof of this Ukrainian Catholic church, announcing its Byzantine origins. Three crosses lift the eye upward, extending the cupolas towards God. Beneath the cupolas and directly above the church's entrance, the facade holds a large mosaic icon that depicts the Annunciation of the Blessed Virgin Mary to which the church is dedicated.

The mosaic's small glittering tiles form an intense image. The icon shows the archangel Gabriel kneeling before Mary to tell her that she is with child. Behind the figures, gold tiles light up the icon, informing the viewer that this is not an earthly scene. This icon, as well as all the stained glass in the church, was designed by Christine Dochwat.

Thick stained-glass windows flank the main entrance but can only be truly appreciated from inside the vestibule. Like the rest of the stained glass in the church, these windows are formed by unusually thick pieces of glass, almost like chunks of intense color. The glass is divided by extremely thick blank bands, making the dark lines of separation as important to the total effect as is the colored glass itself. The final impression is of intense color, angularly presented. This effect becomes more apparent in the nave, where large rectangular panes come together to form the story of Christ's life.

Inside the vestibule, the worshipper immediately recognizes the familiar image of the icon there. For the Ukrainians of the Eastern Rite Church, icons are believed to be the windows of heaven. Icons represent actual people and events. They depict the life of Christ and Mary as well as saints of the Eastern church.

An icon is prepared by one who has fasted for forty days before beginning this spiritual work. The mineral, plant and animal worlds are all represented in the materials the iconographer employs. By using elements of nature for his work, the painter moves closer to God and can, by his finished product, offer the worshipper the same experience.

On the right wall of the vestibule is an icon of Jesus. *"Take courage, I have overcome the world,"* is proclaimed in English and in Ukrainian. Here Christ holds the sun in his right hand and the moon in his

Icon of Christ holding the sun and the moon above rows of votive candles.

left. Above the globes are identifying names. All icons have a way of telling just who and what is being portrayed. Sometimes initials identify the person; sometimes recognizable symbols are included.

Above the door to the nave are the words: *"Peace to those who enter."* The church is considered to be the place where man meets God. Man's experience there, surrounded by the gold icons, is filled with the light of God. The interior of the church is simple, all decorative emphasis being placed on the stained glass and on the iconostasis, or icon screen before the Sanctuary. Rich dark wood has been used for the pews and for the roof which rises to an angle, continuing along the length of the nave.

Surrounding the worshipper are the intensely colored windows. The modern stained glass covers two-thirds of each outside wall. The figures within are formed by these geometric chunks of glass, the irregu-

lar pieces eventually building the angular shapes that are primitive but modern at the same time. The brilliant use of color continues throughout, as though the artist had envisioned pouring paint straight from the tubes without mixing any colors. These jewel-like colors include all hues and, like small building blocks, form powerful pictures that are made more intense by the sun's shining through them.

Christ's story begins on the north wall next to the Sanctuary. In the first window, Mary visits Elizabeth who became the mother of John. It is a poignant scene, as Mary reveals being with child to Elizabeth who has been barren. Now Elizabeth, too, is with child. Zachariah, Elizabeth's husband, witnesses the scene. The background is filled with a simple arch to suggest a building.

The next window is the Nativity, depicting Joseph, Mary and the infant Jesus. The dove, representing the Holy Spirit, soars in the purple sky above the kneeling Mary. In the sky the Star of Bethlehem appears, its golden rays enveloping the Christ child in His cradle. The scene is realistically presented. There is the straw on the floor, and the animals who witness Christ's birth peer from behind a barn door on the right.

Following is the Presentation of Jesus in the Temple. Here Simeon, the High Priest, holds the Child while Anne, Mary and Joseph watch. To the left is a menorah that indicates the building is a synagogue.

On the west wall, beginning again near the Sanctuary, is the Crucifixion followed by the Resurrection. The final window depicts the Ascension into Heaven that occurred forty days after the Resurrection. Here Mary and the Apostles witness the miraculous event. In all these windows, Jesus is the central figure around whom all activity takes place.

At the front of the nave, directly before the iconostasis, is the Tetrapod, a small altar, where the sacraments of matrimony and baptism take place. Notice the intricate cross, enameled with colors, placed here. In the center is the icon of Christ who is surrounded by the four Evangelists: Matthew, Mark, Luke, and John.

There are candles next to icons to the left and right of the Tetrapod. These icons are placed here specifically for veneration as the worshipper respectfully shows reverence for the holy personage represented by the icons. On the right are the Gospels of the

Sacred Scriptures, placed also for veneration.

An understanding of the iconostasis must begin with the doors in the center of the screen. The Royal Doors are an opening used only by the priest during the liturgy. While the altar beyond represents the Father, the doors represent the Son, and the people congregated in worship hold the Holy Spirit within them. On the Royal Doors themselves, are icons of the Annunciation with icons of the four Evangelists below. To the right there are two smaller icons, Christ and St. John Chrysostom, the author of the liturgy, reserved for the veneration of the priest. On the left doors are Mary and St. Basil the Great, who authored another liturgy. At the top of the doors is the depiction of the Last Supper. Notice the figure of Judas Iscariot, the last on the right, who sits with his head turned. His betrayal of Christ is thus shown as he refuses to take part in the meal.

To the right of the Royal Doors (the proper order in which the icons are to be read) is the Icon of Christ the Teacher with a book resting below him that contains a scriptural quotation. Then follows the Deacon Door, where the deacons and altar boys enter the Sanctuary. The last two icons on this side represent the Archangel Gabriel and St. Parascevia, a martyr.

To the left of the Royal Doors are the icons of Mary, the Mother of God, with the infant Jesus beneath her, Archdeacon Stephen, the first martyr, and St. Nicholas, an Archbishop. An interesting aspect of these icons is the symbolic use of color; there is an actual theology of color. Red is understood as the color of divinity while blue is understood to represent humanity. Notice the drapery surrounding the figures of Jesus and Mary. Jesus wears a red undergarment acknowledging his divinity, but as he took on human flesh, he wears on top a blue cloak as a sign of his earthliness.

Mary, on the other hand, was born on earth, so she is shown with a blue undergarment. After her Assumption into heaven, into the eternal world with God, she is then draped in the red outer garment to show her spirituality.

The pattern holds true even in the carpet beneath. In the nave, a blue carpet covers the floor; in the sanctuary, a red carpet is used. The significance is now obvious. Symbolized is the separation between heaven and earth, as the red carpet begins just at the front of the Sanctuary. People come to worship to experience a glimpse of heaven when the Royal Doors are opened for liturgy.

Behind the open-worked brass doors is the Sanctuary where the Sacred Mysteries are celebrated. During the service, the priest always faces east. He is surrounded by more icons that have been painted directly onto the church's walls. High on the center wall is God the Father with the Holy Spirit (in the form of the Dove) and then Jesus depicted beneath Him. Radiating bands link these icons to the others of the Sanctuary, those relating to the Marian feasts on the left and those relating to the Christological feasts on the right. Notice the ray that shoots downward ending only above a large chair. This chair is the Bishop's Throne, acknowledging the Bishop's role as representative of the Father.

Altar with Tabernacle, ripidia, processional cross, and icons representing God, the Holy Spirit and Jesus.

To the left is a table called the Proskomedia where the Eucharist is prepared. To the right, the Diaconicon Table is situated where the priest dons the liturgical vestments. Directly center is the Altar where the Tabernacle, containing the blessed sacrament, is placed. Behind stand icons surrounded by starburst ripidia or fans that, along with the tall cross next to them, are used for processions.

The architecture of this church is not typically Byzantine, but the interior identifies it as an Eastern Rite Church. The church reaches back to Constantinople for its religious tradition, keeping its own form of worship and language alive in this country. As part of an awareness of Ukrainian culture, the church has formed a parish choir that performs at cultural events in the area.

The people of the Church of Annunciation pray here today as they have for twenty-eight years, facing the glittering red candles and the brilliance of the iconostatis. Surrounded by the impact of the massive glass windows, their pattern of worship continues. For many this church has become a place where heaven meets earth, where men and women, who have made themselves open to the spiritual, can welcome God.

St. John's Evangelical Lutheran Church

St. John's Evangelical Lutheran Church

Corner of Old York Road and Melrose Avenue, Melrose Park

HISTORY

At the dawn of the twentieth century, a migration of city residents to the outlying suburb of Cheltenham Township was well under way. Lutherans, who had a long and established relationship with inner-city parishes were now interested in forming new congregations west and north of Philadelphia's boundaries.

In 1902, with the energetic assistance of the Rev. Charles G. Spieker, Dr. J. Frederick Herbert and Mr. E. Clarence Miller encouraged a number of Lutheran families to organize St. John's Evangelical Lutheran Church. Charter members met for worship in Ogontz Hall as Rev. Spieker accepted the call to become the congregation's first pastor on January 19, 1902. Shortly thereafter, a constitution was adopted, and on February 10, 1902 a State Charter was granted.

With a rapidly growing program and ever-increasing membership, a larger property was needed. The gift of building lots by Mr. William Elkins at Stahr Road and Park Avenue, Ogontz, enabled the congregation to proceed with the construction of their first church building. The doors were opened to the community in the spring of 1904.

Pastor Spieker tendered his resignation in March of 1910, and a new era of pastoral leadership began with The Rev. Charles J. Gable in August of that same year. Membership continued to increase rapidly and the congregation gave serious consideration to acquiring a more accessible and prominent location. The existing structure was sold to the Christian Science Church as Mr. E. Clarence Miller provided a new site at the corner of Old York Road and Melrose Ave., Melrose Park. Just twelve years after the first service in cramped Ogontz Hall, the members of St. John's dedicated their new spacious facility to the glory of God on April 13, 1913.

The next two decades were years of expansion and growth for St. John's. Dr. Ernest T. Allen became full-time organist and choir director, serving the congregation for thirty-nine years. Along with the initiation of mid-week Lenten services in 1922, St. John's ministry grew with the establishment of the Men's Brotherhood and a Saturday morning Bible class. The tripling of attendance in just twenty years caused vestry members to consider further expansion of the church's facilities.

After twenty-one years of distinguished service, Pastor Gable resigned in January, 1931, due to illness. The Rev. Frederick Nolde served as Interim Pastor until the congregation called the Rev. Kenneth P. Otten on January 17, 1932. Dr. Otten's commitment to visitation and evangelism bore fruit in an ever-growing membership and an expanding program of ministry. One such area of growth included the founding of the Women's Auxiliary in 1934. Previous to this time, the Ladies Aid Society was instrumental in supporting the church both financially and socially. Through their considerable efforts, the congregation actively participated in the development of St. John's life and mission. The history of the parish reflects the ongoing strength of various women's organizations. Along with the Ladies Aid Society, the Missionary Society and Auxiliary, St. John's has been blessed with an active Lutheran Church Women's program. Both the Rachel and Ruth Circles have provided opportunities for Christian witness and service for ladies of all ages and interests.

Thoughts turned to the redecoration of the chancel and sanctuary areas of the church, and in 1942 the present marble and French caen stone altar and reredos were donated as memorials. A general renovation of the worship room followed which included the decorative treatment of the chancel ceiling.

After thirty-three years of faithful service to the

Lord, Dr. Otten announced his retirement in 1965. He remained as "Pastor Emeritus" until his death in 1985. The reins of leadership were passed to the Rev. Jan C. Walker who was installed on October 11, 1964. His friendly and out-going personality was the catalyst for another era of growth and development within the congregation and throughout the community.

Of special importance were the installation of a new Moller pipe organ and the construction of a second addition to the Parish House. These physical improvements paved the way for an expanded music and Christian Education program.

Following Pastor Walker's tenure, The Rev. Charles A. Gills was installed as the congregation's new pastor on December 14, 1969. Under his leadership membership continued to grow as did interest in a variety of outreach ministries. Close contact with Center City Lutheran parishes developed, and the members of St. John's were able to provide staple goods for food pantries and robes for youth choirs. The Committee of Concern was re-established to aid the sick and shut-ins, and the Sunday services were recorded and shared with those unable to attend church. A bus ministry was introduced and various men's and women's organizations further developed their programs.

In November of 1978 Pastor Gills resigned, and in August of 1979 the Rev. E. Carl Zimmermann began his ministry at St. John's. The congregation enjoyed modest growth, and additional staff members were hired to assist in the church's expanding program. Of special note was the introduction of the Lutheran Book of Worship which provides a common focal point of celebration for over five million Lutherans throughout the United States. The congregation also celebrated its eighty-fifth anniversary in 1987. The year long festivities were marked by special music, guest preachers and a gala banquet.

Strengthened by a vibrant past, the members of St. John's look ahead to a promising future. They have been blessed from the very beginning of their history with strong and capable pastoral and lay leadership. They have a keen sense of their rich heritage and have committed themselves to God's service within the walls of their church and throughout the community.

*"Here Jesus walks among
His flock. In His arms is the lost lamb…"*

St. John's Evangelical Lutheran Church

While St. John's Lutheran Church dates from 1913, the congregation was organized in 1902. The exterior of the stone church hints at its Gothic origins. Bells were originally hung in the tall tower, but now the tradition is continued by an electronic carillon that chimes on the hour. At certain hours during the day, the carillon plays traditional hymns, sending forth the strains of rich music as the bells had done in the past.

The original church is now part of a complex of buildings. The Sacristy was added after 1913, another extension was added in 1946, and the Parish building was added in 1964 and today houses an active preschool program. Within these many rooms the congregation offers opportunities for Christian education, social outreach and fellowship.

The interior of the church is both simple and richly detailed at the same time. The walls above the green tiled wainscoting are painted a pure white. There are three large stained glass windows in the church as well as a number of smaller ones that are filled with abstract designs. However, it is the power of dark wood that first impresses the visitor. The wooden pews are darkly stained as are the hammer-headed wooden trusses of the roof above. But the pews, the pulpit, the lectern and the half wall that surrounds the choir in the chancel are intricately carved. Pointed arches within rectangles are etched into the wood, providing a richness of design, as well as carrying on the Gothic mood of the church.

The heavy wooden support beams of the ceiling dip down into the interior of the church. The beams rest solidly upon white plaster brackets that extend from the walls. Yet as massive as the wooden beams appear to be, the ceiling above them soars into the pitch traditional in Gothic churches. The beams that stretch horizontally across the nave have an openness that is produced by the many support beams coming together at a single point. The same contrasting sense of weight but lightness occurs in the chancel. This area appears dramatically set off from the rest of the church as it begins after the break of a solid white wall. Within the pentagonally shaped extension, the roof seems a separate entity that follows the pattern of the nave, but could almost stand alone.

Large brass chandeliers hang from the beams providing light in addition to the windows. The lighting fixtures are interesting as they reflect the time in which the church was built. Above the electric globes, gas jets curl upward. When electricity failed, illumination was still possible as each individual jet was then lit. Most of the church appointments have been retained in original form, maintaining the atmosphere of the period in which the church was constructed.

On the west wall of the nave, the large Ascension window powerfully declares this element of the Christ story. Flanked by smaller windows depicting from left to right, the angels Uriel, Michael, Raphael, and Gabriel, the Ascension dominates this part of the church. In the upper half of the window, the lacy spires of a Gothic cathedral stretch upwards. Notice the two angels in the upper corners who watch the scene below them. The window is made up of five panels, with Jesus taking His place in the central panel. The three women who had gone to the Sepulcher kneel before him turning completely towards the rising Christ. Two angels on either side, unlike the women, face forward but turn their heads towards the miracle. Behind the figures are the rich hues of a forest, the deep blues and greens surrounding Jesus. The heads of cherubim peek from among the trees as the emissaries of heaven take part in the earthly scene.

The five-panel Ascension Window.

formal in the approach to the story it tells, and more detailed in depicting a scene from nature. Here Jesus walks among His flock. In His arms is the lost lamb that He has found and is returning to the others. Christ gently holds the lamb, gazing at it while clasping it to His body.

There is a sense of movement in the window as the animals surround Jesus. He walks barefooted. The sheep are caught in slow motion, hooves just about to be placed, heads just about to turn. Their bodies are given dimension by the suggestion of perspective. Purple hills roll across the left background capturing a city that sits by the banks of a lake. Tracings of trees and buildings are visible. In the foreground there is the hint of a stone building on the right. Jesus walks on rocks and green leaves and wears the only brilliant color in the window: a scarlet cloak.

On the right side of the church near the Chancel, is the Baptistry. Set behind a separate stone archway, the font is placed within its own area. The marble font has a brass cover that is engraved with the dove and the cross. Around the circumference are clam shells

The figures are realistically portrayed. There are the intricate modeling of the bodies, the detail of the faces, and the richness of the draperies that suggest brocade and pattern. The angels' wings stretch behind them in brilliant red with each feather outlined and defined. But among all this richness of color and design, the figure of Christ captures all attention. By contrast, He is a pale shape, but one that actually glows within the scene. His white body is draped in pale green robes as He slips off the white shroud of His burial. Behind Him, blue light radiates from heaven to illuminate Christ as He ascends.

The transept of the church is suggested by walls that extend the nave slightly to the left and the right. The area is further defined by the large windows that mark the north and south areas of the church. Matthew, Mark, Luke and John, the writers of the Gospels, are the subjects portrayed in the north transept.

Opposite them, in the south window, is a portrayal of Jesus as the Good Shepherd. The window seems different from the others in the church, somewhat less

Baptistry

that signify the Apostles as fishers of men. Three angels, two with musical instruments, are set into narrow stained-glass windows in the rear of this extension, allowing light to filter into the area. Notice the two stone cherubim with their childlike faces that are set into the walls of the dividing archway itself.

Paraments, cloths of different colors that announce the holiday or liturgical season on the church calendar, hang from the pulpit, lectern and altar. Embroidered with Christian symbols, the paraments are changed as occasion demands with blue representing the Advent season, white symbolizing Christmas, green employed for the seasons of Epiphany and Pentecost, purple for Lent and red hung on special Sundays.

Pass by the organ (which has undergone improvements recently) to the altar. Notice the complete symmetry of this area, the white marble altar surrounded by small windows whose colors are transformed by the open stone work in front of them. Two candelabra flank the altar. Rising high on the east wall is the Reredos, the tall, caen stone extension above the altar that was added in the 1940s. Within the carved backdrop are four statues representing the four Gospel writers. Elongated, narrow forms that fit within the pointed niches behind them, the statues are reminiscent of sculpture that often flanks the doorways of Gothic cathedrals in Europe.

Notice the other details in the Chancel. Painted wood runs around the perimeter of the ceiling, and red and black shields containing other Christian symbols hang on the wooden beams.

But within this area is the most powerful window in the church: the Crucifixion window which hangs directly opposite the Ascension window of the west wall. Above the altar, the small window is set deeply into the east wall, the depth increased by the Reredos that sits in front of it. The window itself is the shape of the Cross. There are no borders, no background scene, no extra details of any sort. Simply and powerfully, Christ hangs on His cross.

Within this dark Gothic church, with its massive ceiling and large windows, this small portrayal of Jesus at the moment of death dominates. Somehow the eye is drawn forward, and even when viewed from the west wall, the Crucifixion seems the focus of the church. When the lights are extinguished, this window actually glows.

St. John's has preserved the church as it was when it was first built. Those who worshipped here in 1913 welcomed the additional space their growing community demanded and filled the Gothic interior with thanks and song. Today the church community continues what was begun at the turn of the century. This dramatic church is the focal point of their worship.

Chancel, with altar, reredos and Crucifixion window.

Congregation Adath Jeshurun

Congregation Adath Jeshurun

Corner of Old York Road and Ashbourne Road, Elkins Park

HISTORY*

The founding of Adath Jeshurun in 1858 brought to seven the number of Jewish congregations in Philadelphia. Mikve Israel, the oldest, had been founded in 1745, Rodeph Shalom in 1795, Beth Israel in 1840 and Keneseth Israel in 1847. Two other congregations founded in the 1850s disbanded before the turn of the century. There were approximately 50,000 Jews in the United States by the mid-1850s, and more than ten percent lived in Philadelphia.

The founding fathers of Adath Jeshurun, Wolf Ettinger and Moses Blumenthal, realized that education was of prime importance for children. They felt that the younger generation needed to learn Hebrew and English, as well as German. Most of the members of the new congregation were of German extraction due to the wave of German immigration which flooded America in the 1850s. For many years the minutes of the meetings of Adath Jeshurun's executive committee were taken in both English and German. The new congregation began meeting in Union Hall at Third and Brown Streets on April 16, 1859.

In 1865, under the leadership of Dr. S. Nathans, a synagogue was purchased at the corner of Newmarket and Noble Streets. During his tenure, a permanent *hazzan* (cantor) was retained. Nathans continued as rabbi until 1869, when the *hazzan*, Reverend Moses E. Cohen, became teacher, cantor and spiritual leader. Cohen introduced choir music into the Divine Service in 1873. As the congregation grew, it was decided to purchase a new house of worship. The congregation moved to its Juliana Street Synagogue in 1875.

In August, 1883, Reverend Elias Eppstein was elected Rabbi and Cantor. It was decided that, in

*Adapted from a history edited by Marvin Shore and Charlotte Viner Bernstein

addition to innovations being made in the form of the service and method of seating, other changes of a "progressive conservative" nature were needed. First, there was the installation of a magnificent organ in 1876, and in 1883 another step toward reform was taken with the institution of late Friday evening services.

In the 1880s Philadelphia and many other cities in the United States experienced an enormous influx of Jews fleeing the virulence of anti-Semitism in Eastern Europe. Over two million Jews found refuge in the United States between 1880 and the outbreak of the First World War. As Adath Jeshurun continued to grow, it became necessary to build a new and still larger synagogue. In 1886, a lot at Seventh Street and Columbia Avenue was purchased as the site for the new building. Events moved smoothly, and at Sabbath Evening services, on Friday, September 24th, 1886, just before the High Holy Days, the new building was officially dedicated.

During this period, Adath Jeshurun began slowly moving toward the Reform movement. The new rabbi, Rev. Elias Eppstein who came to Adath Jeshurun from Kansas City, began the practice of delivering sermons regularly. Eppstein was succeeded by Rabbi Henry Illowizi in 1888. Thirteen years later in 1901, Rabbi Bernard C. Ehrenreich came to Adath Jeshurun and remained until 1906. At that time Rabbi Jacob H. Landau took the pulpit, having completed a fourteen year record of success in England and Australia.

With the resignation of Rabbi Landau in February, 1910, the congregation found itself without spiritual leadership as the High Holy Days approached. To fill the pulpit, it was necessary to retain the services of a promising young rabbinical student. Thus Rabbi Max D. Klein, who served Adath Jeshurun until 1960, began his distinguished half-century of leadership. In

1911, a turning point for the congregation, the building at Seventh and Columbia was sold and a new synagogue was constructed at Broad and Diamond. At the same time Rabbi Klein set a clear direction for the congregation toward Conservative Judaism.

During Rabbi Klein's tenure, the congregation became involved in the many world-wide issues affecting Jews. Problems within the city, including a furor over the cost of kosher meat in Philadelphia, also demanded his attention. The congregation continued to grow to such proportions that it became necessary to build a new Auditorium and School building. Under Rabbi Klein's leadership, Adath Jeshurun became one of the founding congregations of the United Synagogue of America, the congregational arm of American Conservative Judaism.

As Adath Jeshurun's rate of growth accelerated in the aftermath of World War II, a special meeting was held in 1948 to consider the advisability of moving the congregation to a location in the northern section of the city. The bulk of the Adath Jeshurun families with children enrolled in the school were already living in that area. In 1949, two school buildings were in operation. During the week, school was held for some in Melrose Park at York Road and Ainsley Avenue, and others attended school at the Broad and Diamond building.

In 1957, a ten-acre tract at Ashbourne and York Roads was purchased as the site for the erection of a new synagogue and school. This was the initial step in the congregation's ultimate realization of its new building and expansion program. In 1960, Rabbi Klein announced his decision to retire after serving the synagogue with distinction for fifty years. Rabbi Yaakov G. Rosenberg then assumed the post.

The year 1964 witnessed the long awaited move to York and Ashbourne Roads. On Thursday evening, August 18, 1964, Adath Jeshurun took leave of the synagogue at Broad and Diamond Streets, its home for 53 years. Rabbi Rosenberg led the congregation until 1978 when he left to become the Vice Chancellor of the Jewish Theological Seminary of America in New York. He was succeeded by Rabbi Seymour S. Rosenbloom who leads the congregation today. Cantor Charles Davidson, one of America's leading synagogue composers, is Music Director and Hazzan.

The history of Adath Jeshurun extends over a period of eleven decades. It is the vibrant story of a congregational family encompassing a way of life envisioned by the Prophet Micah: *"to do justly, love mercy, and walk humbly with thy God."* At Adath Jeshurun the relevance of the Jewish tradition is linked to the congregants' daily lives as Jews, as Americans, and as human beings.

In the Sanctuary the eye is drawn forward,
towards the focus of every synagogue, towards the Ark.

Congregation Adath Jeshurun

TOUR

In 1964 the cornerstone of the new building of Congregation Adath Jeshurun was laid to proclaim the purpose of this synagogue: *"To Help Perfect the World Under the Kingdom of the Almighty."* Thus this building became a *Bet Am*, a house of the people, that would fulfill three functions, becoming a place of prayer, of study, and of assembly.

The modern flavor of this building is immediately apparent. The synagogue is set along horizontal lines, with the central entrance placed beneath an upward tilt of the roof line. This angular, upward movement is repeated inside the sanctuary itself. Unlike churches which traditionally follow the cruciform in structure, the synagogue can take any form. Historically, synagogue architecture copied the styles of the country in which the building existed. There have been Byzantine, Moorish, and Classical synagogues through the centuries.

Adath Jeshurun houses many classrooms for religious study as well as two Sanctuaries for prayer. During the year the synagogue also offers a Hebraic art series that is open to the community.

Before entering, notice the massive Menorahs that stand on either side of the main door. Executed by the sculptor Chaim Gross, they stand ready to be lit in welcome. These differ somewhat from the typically seven-limbed Menorahs usually found inside most synagogues. Here nine candles adorn the bronze candelabrum signifying Chanukah, the Festival of Lights. There is one light for each of the eight days of the holiday, and one additional light, the *Shamash*, that traditionally lights the others.

Large panels of stained glass windows flank the entrance. At this point the windows appear simply composed of dark lines and filled only with white glass. Their beauty can be appreciated once inside the vestibule. The windows, again modern in their treat-

One of two Chaim Gross Menorahs flanking main entrance.

ment, become alive with color. Designed by Efrem Weitzman, they echo predominant religious themes: Torah, Worship, Righteousness, Truth, Justice and Peace. The world is believed to be founded on the first three concepts and maintained by the last three. In these windows colors cut into the white background in tall, narrow bands so filled with movement that they dance within the strong vertical space. There is tremendous energy here that is visible only from inside.

The vestibule of the synagogue serves the purpose of transition for the worshipper as he moves from the

Daroff Chapel with Ark and Decalogue.

outside world to the concentrated experience of the Sanctuary. At Adath Jeshurun there is the Daroff Chapel to visit as well as the main Sanctuary. The Chapel is used for daily services, housing the morning and evening prayers. Here the worshipper is surrounded by stained glass windows, also designed by Efrem Weitzman, that capture the meaning of the eight major Jewish holidays and festivals: Rosh Hashanah, Yom Kippur, Sukkot, Chanukah, Purim, Passover, and Shavuot. Five more thematic windows were added that reflect holiday themes.

There are many entrances to the Main Sanctuary, but above the center two doors hangs the *Ner Tamid*, the Eternal Light, that usually hangs in front of the Ark within. This Light was taken from the old synagogue when the congregation moved to the present building. It reflects a less modern style of design, with its open worked brass and the lacy filagree of metal, surrounding a light heightened by red glass. This Eternal Light is part of the continuing tradition of the congregation.

When you enter the main Sanctuary, a single, large room, you will stand at the widest part of a narrowing semicircle. The rows of wooden pews, the inward direction of the aisles, and the angled edges of the

Eternal Light, from former Synagogue in North Philadelphia.

circle itself draw the eye forward, towards the focus of every synagogue, the Ark. Notice the simplicity of the Sanctuary. The walls are made of wood that circles to fabric-covered panels and finally to the massive marble slabs that flank the Ark itself. Color here is found in the Ark doors and in the stained glass windows that flow next to the roof line and extend the entire length of the sanctuary.

The roof itself soars. There is the upward movement, hinted at with the building's entrance that is continued here. The ceiling, which begins on an angle to the outward walls to slant dramatically upward, is composed of many levels that bring the roof line higher and higher. There is the gap between the first ceiling level and the next that is produced by the stained glass and raises the ceiling even more, culminating in full height above the Ark. Even here the ceiling angles, forming a "V". The effect is a dramatic sense of elongation, where the total impact of height comes directly above the Ark.

The platform on which three wooden desks are situated is called the *bima*. Originally, the *bima* held the desk where the Torah, the scroll containing the five books of Moses, would be placed during the service and read aloud to the congregation. Historically the reader's table was often located opposite the Ark in the middle of the congregation. Congregants would sit on chairs or benches around the reader's table. In modern times the reader's table is usually situated near the lecterns used by the Rabbi and the Cantor. In this synagogue the table has been purposely situated on a lower level than the other two lecterns in an attempt to read the Torah from among the people, following the ancient tradition.

Behind the lecterns are three steps that echo the words "*Holy, Holy, Holy*" repeated in ancient times as the priests moved from one sacred chamber to the next, closer and closer to the Sanctuary where the Ark was held. The Torah Ark, *Aron ha-Kodesh*, reflects the ancient Holy of Holies in the Biblical temple. Originally, the Ark was free-standing, but the modern tradition has been to recess it into the east wall of the Sanctuary, into the wall closest to Jerusalem. Within, in an upright position, rest the synagogue's nine Torahs on two tiers. The Torah scrolls, often dressed in velvet covers, their handles covered by silver Torah crowns, a silver breast plate draped

across the front, are the most sacred items in all synagogues. In fact, all a synagogue really needs is a single Torah scroll. When the Ark is opened during a service and the Torahs are revealed, the worshipers in front are dwarfed. Thus the architect has suggested the importance of the Torahs that hold the word of God as revealed to Moses.

The Torahs are kept behind colorful Ark doors. Historically the Ark curtains were embroidered in rich colors on velvet or silk. Following this tradition, these doors were first designed by Sam Maitin, a local artist, and then the pattern was transferred onto canvas to be done by needlepoint. Many women and men of the congregation labored to produce the total effect. Intense colors swirl boldly upwards.

The design of the Ark flows upward towards the Eternal Light and towards the rendition of the Ten Commandments. These brass sculptures, as well as the Menorah that hangs to the right of the Ark, were designed by Maxwell M. Chayat. The Eternal Light signifies the Divine Presence, repeating the appearance of God to Moses through the burning bush, but it also represents the permanence of the Torah and its teachings. The light burns at all times within its modern, brass web. Open bands encircle the copper-colored light that forms the only solid mass. This openness is repeated in the Tablets that hang above it, where the Laws are lightly outlined in thin brass and the Hebrew letters jump forward in stronger contrast. The Commandments remind the worshipper of his duty to man and to God.

The Menorah to the right also echoes the brass open-work. Brass bands curl around and behind the candles, almost cupping their flames in reflective metal. There is an extension to the Menorah that adds an additional candle for Chanukah services.

The use of the seven-limbed Menorah in the religious tradition can be traced to one made by Bezalel for the Tabernacle in the desert during Moses' wanderings. After the second century, the Menorah appeared in synagogues. In modern synagogues the Menorah takes many forms that, while containing the same seven limbs, also reflect the imagination of the sculptor and the materials he has chosen to use.

To enjoy the stained glass clerestory windows designed by Karel Dupre, you will have to shift positions as both are not visible at the same time. Both windows begin as narrow bands that contain simple colors. The design finally bursts into space and vibrancy when the complicated swirling patterns intensify as they move towards the Ark.

Before leaving the Sanctuary, stand again by the vestibule wall. Notice the stark simplicity of the Sanctuary where all elements, the inward radiating aisles, the expanding energy of the stained glass, the raising of the roof line, and the elevation of the *bima* itself lead the eye to the colorfully defined, massive Ark. The symbolic power of the Ark and the Torahs it holds are all important here. For the worshipper, all attention is focused on the front of the Sanctuary as he, himself, stands in awe.

St. Paul's Episcopal Church

St. Paul's Episcopal Church

Old York Road and Ashbourne Road, Elkins Park

HISTORY

On an evening in June of 1860, twelve men, the first Vestry of St. Paul's Church, met at the home of Jay Cooke in Cheltenham. These men wanted a church closer to their new homes, as the trip to St. Paul's on Third Street near Spruce in the city was considered too far to travel. The purpose of the meeting was to plan the building of a church on a lot of ground at the corner of Old York Road and Ashbourne Road. The church was to be called "Saint Paul's Church of Cheltenham".

The cornerstone was laid on September 3, 1860, and on May 16, 1861, the church was solemnly consecrated by Rev. Alonzo Potter. On Witsunday, 1861, the church was opened for services.

The first Rector of St. Paul's was the Rev. Robert J. Parvin. During his tenure a new organ was placed in the church and the Sunday School was enlarged to house the Men's Bible Class and the Infant School. The Rt. Rev. William Bacon Stevens confirmed the first class of fifteen persons in 1862. Mr. Parvin resigned in 1866.

The Rev. Edward W. Appleton was elected Rector of St. Paul's in June of 1867. In the more than thirty-one years that Mr. Appleton was Rector, many additions and improvements were made to the church. In 1868 the Rectory was completed and occupied. The tower with bell, clock and chime of ten bells, and the transept were added to the church building. In 1879 the grounds lying east of the church were designated for burial purposes. The Rev. Mr. Appleton was elected Rector Emeritus in 1899 and died in 1901. He was succeeded by the Rev. J. Thompson Cole, the third Rector of St. Paul's Church.

At the turn of the century, apart from the morning and evening services, the work of the Parish was carried on by four Bible Classes and a Sunday School. There was also a Parish Aid Society, a Circle of the King's Daughters, a Woman's Auxiliary, and a sewing school. Services were attended by students from the Cheltenham Military Academy and the Ogontz Seminary.

In 1905, Jay Cooke died after forty-five years of devoted service to his church. Mr. Cooke was the first teacher of the Men's Bible Class and was Rector's Warden for twenty-three years. As a memorial to him, his heirs erected Jay Cooke Memorial Hall, a permanent home for the Men's Bible Class.

With the death of the Rev. Mr. Cole in 1917, the Rev. Philip J. Steinmetz, Jr., was elected Rector. Many contributions were made to the church during the twenty-seven years of Dr. Steinmetz's tenure. The sexton's house was built as a memorial to Laura E. C. Barney; the chancel was rebuilt; radio station WIBG was installed; the name of the church was changed from St. Paul's of Cheltenham to St. Paul's of Elkins Park; and an Endowment Fund was established.

The Rev. Philip Humason Steinmetz, son of the Rector, was elected assistant to the Rector in 1934, and in 1946, following the death of Dr. Steinmetz, the Vestry elected the Rev. Frederic R. Murray as Rector. During Mr. Murray's Rectorship the number of communicants grew, the budget was increased, and improvements were made to the church. The Evening Auxiliary, Young People's Groups, Church School Choir, Athletic Association, and Boy Scout Troop were formed. The Rev. Mr. Murray resigned in 1955.

The Rev. James G. Ludwig III assumed his duties as St. Paul's sixth Rector on All Saints Day, 1955. The first five years of the Rev. Mr. Ludwig's ministry at St. Paul's were a time of considerable progress. Among the more noteworthy events were the formation of the Parish Council, the organization of Lay Readers and the Church Office Guild of volunteer workers, the institution of mid-week Thursday evening services of Holy Communion and Divine Healing and the Family Service on Sunday mornings.

A "Five Year Plan" was adopted by the Vestry with an eye towards the Centennial Celebration in 1961. This plan consisted of additions and improvements to the existing church property. On May 17, 1959 the Livezey Memorial Chapel of Intercession was dedicated.

The Langsdorf property, fronting on York Road and adjoining the church property on the north, was purchased in 1957. The main building on this property was known as the Parish House, and it housed the church office, the Rector's office, and church school rooms.

The Rev. Albutt Gardner succeeded Rev. Ludwig in 1970 and served until 1982. Mr. Gardner led St. Paul's Church through the difficult transition of the Episcopal Church in the '70s. A new Book of Common Prayer was introduced, and the issue of the ordination of women was addressed. The '70s were indeed a tumultuous time for the Episcopal Church.

In 1983, Rev. L. Denver Hart was called as the eighth Rector of the parish. Under his leadership the parish celebrated its 125th anniversary and was able to undertake a major capital fund drive. Rev. Hart resigned after a call to Manhattan's St. Bartholemew's Church in March, 1990. As we go to press, Rev. Richard Schmidt is serving as Interim Pastor, and the search for a new pastor is beginning.

In recent years an Early Childhood Center was added to St. Paul's. Founded as a quiet country parish in Civil War days, St. Paul's continues to serve and to meet the needs of the community with distinction today.

The walls of this "English country church"
are punctuated by thirteen exquisite Tiffany windows.

St. Paul's Episcopal Church

TOUR

St. Paul's is the oldest church building in the town of Cheltenham. This "country church," reminiscent of small churches all through west England, is admired not only for the beauty of its stained glass windows by Willet, Kolls, Reith, and most especially, by Louis Comfort Tiffany, but also for the history the building captures. It was not until 1982 that St. Paul's was added to the National Register of Historic Places, but its story goes back to 1860 when it was founded by Jay Cooke.

The original church, designed and expanded three times by James C. Sidney who also designed St. Paul's of Chestnut Hill, served most of the prosperous nineteenth-century families of the area: the Elkins, the Wideners and their circle. These were the people who moved out of the city to build grand homes and eventually to build their own churches.

There is a church and a chapel at St. Paul's. The Livezey Chapel of the Intercession was designed in 1959 by James G. Lugwig, the rector of the church who had once been an architect. It is used for weddings and funerals as well as for Morning Prayer. Lugwig designed the altar rail and the delicately patterned wrought iron cross. The cross depicts the five petitions of prayer. The three stained glass panels on the left are by Willet Studios.

Move from this chapel, passing beneath the church's bell and clock tower built in 1869 by the young ladies of the parish, and into the narthex, which was added to celebrate the 100th anniversary of the church. It is here that the first evidence of Jay Cooke's powerful presence can be found. Cooke's desk, marked with a plaque, sits against the outside wall. It was on this desk that the wealthy financier worked during the Civil War, underwriting the bonds that provided the North with monetary backing.

Cooke, a great lover of the Bible, taught religious

Jay Cooke's desk in narthex.

classes as well as being a major church benefactor. His memory is caught at other points in the building. There is an inscription that lists Cooke's contributions on the north wall just before the pulpit. The church yard, a veritable "Who's Who" of the wealthy families in the area, holds Cooke's mausoleum which resembles Moorish architecture. The structure originally rested on the grounds of Cooke's nearby home, "Ogontz," but was moved to the graveyard when the Wideners bought his land.

When you enter the nave from the narthex, you will immediately feel the Gothic mood of the church. The windows rise to points; the hammer-head wooden trusses cross overhead. The walls have been scored to resemble caen stone. And yet the church is a simple one, most of the decoration provided by the exquisite Tiffany windows that punctuate the stone walls. Turn around, just as you enter the nave, to find the final tribute to Cooke, added a year after his death in 1905 by the Young Ladies of Ogontz School who sat in the balcony (since removed) below the window. Here St. Paul, in a vibrant salmon robe typical of Tiffany's skill with color, preaches and builds young churches in Athens, as Cooke had built his church in Cheltenham.

There are thirteen Tiffany windows to enjoy in the church, but two in the nave bear special attention. In 1914, George and Harry Widener, father and son, died on the S.S. *Titanic* with their manservant. Mrs. Eleanor (Elkins) Widener and her maid survived. They had visited Europe to buy a trousseau for George's daughter (who later became Mrs. Fitz Eugene Dixon) and to purchase books for Harry's collection. An

enthusiastic bibliophile, Harry owned a Gutenburg Bible and was said to have been carrying a gold and jewel encrusted copy of the *Rubaiyat* of Omar Khayyam when the ship sank.

The window on the south wall, second from the west end door, was given in Widener's memory. Here a young St. John the Evangelist looks to God for inspiration to write his *Revelations*, the massive book held in his left hand. There is action even in the stillness of the window, as the saint is caught at the moment of spiritual inspiration. The foliage of blues and greens and the suggested peaks behind him are there only as background for the figure illuminated by knowledge.

The window dedicated to George Widener is on the north wall, next to the Cooke plaque and second from the pulpit. Here the relationship to the *Titanic* disaster is more powerfully felt. Jesus as shepherd stands with staff in hand. The other hand is open and

Tiffany windows, depicting St. John and Jesus, dedicated to the memories of George and Henry Elkins Widener.

welcoming at His side. At first glance, there are blue mountains in the background. But if you look closely, you will see outlines of water and ice. There was Jesus, in the desolate land that surrounded the dying of the *Titanic*, waiting. Behind the blue ice, light radiates upward, illuminating the once dark sky. For the Wideners, whose death prompted these windows and the great Widener Library at Harvard, as well as for the others who died on board the *Titanic*, the window testifies to Jesus' presence at death.

Across from this window, past the Gothic rood screen that was added as a memorial to the men who died during World War II, is the transept, added in 1887, which at one time housed the Elkins organ and the choir. Here are other Tiffany Windows; one is dedicated to a fallen hero of World War I, Frederick George Wilmsen. In romantic, chivalric images, a youth, wearing a laurel wreath as testimony to his bravery, kneels. His sword is laid gently at his side as clouds swirl around and beneath him in Tiffany's expression of heaven. Before him, the Angel of Victory emerges from the clouds to bestow honor on him. The clouds begin as lavender bands and dissolve to white as light fills the top of the window.

This window is typical of Tiffany's work. Like other members of the Pre-Raphaelite movement, Tiffany attempted to restore purity of hand craftsmanship in a time when the emerging dominance of the machine was viewed as a threat. For Tiffany, the challenge came in stained glass and often in windows for churches. The windows became an art form as he created ambitious images and developed new methods of working with glass. Here you can see that sheets of glass have been overlaid to produce an intense impact of color. In the darker areas, as many as five sheets of glass may have been used. The intricacy of the angel's wings contribute to the volume of the angel herself, and the drapery that surrounds her is made of glass that has been buckled or folded to produce a three-dimensional effect. The other major Tiffany windows are in memory of William Elkins, Stella Elkins Tyler and Caleb Fox.

Turn now and walk towards the altar of the church. You will pass the organ facade, added by P.A.B. Widener after he heard the organ of St. Bartholomew's

in New York. Across the ceiling, in the chancel designed by Horace Trumbauer, painted wooden trusses are anchored by cherubim faces. Along the east wall sits the simple altar donated by the Wideners, along with the altar rail, linens and silver in memory of Harry and George Widener. It is made of the same caen stone used to build the castles of medieval Europe. The altar with its stone angels was kept simple, for the Wideners would send potted palms and flowers from their home each Sunday for decoration.

Above the altar is one of the most beautiful Tiffany windows in the church, the church's earliest window. Dedicated in 1897 in memory of P.A.B. Widener's late wife, it was also the first addition to the church by Trumbauer. Trumbauer rebuilt the entire front of the church to accommodate this window, all at the expense of Mr. Widener. Here, Jesus, on the morning of the Resurrection, rises. Mary Magdelene is to His right; angels bearing witness kneel to His left. Jesus is the apex of a triangle of figures, as he appears to be all in light. Behind him, the sun rises in the east. The folds of fabric are produced again by actual folds in the glass itself. Jesus' face is intricately painted, as is Mary's. In the dark background which serves to highlight the figures, cherubim float above, looking down and at each other. It is a scene both of heaven and earth.

The memorial plaque to the World War I servicemen reads like a "Who's Who" of the York Road social scene of 1920. The brass lectern and pulpit date from the early 1900s and were donated in memory of the early ministers of the Church. Electricity was run from Mr. Roelof's dynamos across York Road to light the church and rectory in 1887.

Before you leave the church think of the times that have passed. Imagine the early parishioners arriving by horse and carriage, worshiping by candle and gas light, the men and women who moved by the pews that still bear their names, the silk of the women's dresses testifying to the wealth that developed the area. Remember the country's fighting the Civil War when many church women ministered to the wounded at Antietam and Gettysburg. Imagine the Vestry meetings in the Rectory, the superb "Cottage Gothic"

Chancel with large Tiffany window depicting Jesus on the morning of the Resurrection.

Victorian mansion built and donated by Jay Cooke and his brother-in-law Morehead in 1868, where Jay Cooke, Elkins, Widener, Roelof (Stetson's son-in-law), Barney (Cooke's son-in-law) and other millionaires were seated in the Rector's study and were in deep discussions about church finances.

Today acts of charity continue as the church fosters support for the Wharton Centre for the Homeless by providing basics as well as funds. But the history of people and of the area is always linked to St. Paul's. Think of the service for the *Titanic* and the shock the disaster must have produced in the community. In the beauty of St. Paul's there are always reminders of the past.

Church of the Annunciation

Church of the Annunciation
(Greek Orthodox)
921 Old York Road, Elkins Park

HISTORY

When the Greek Orthodox parish was being organized in Philadelphia back at the turn of the century, only five other such parishes existed on the American continent: New Orleans (1804), two in New York City (1892 and 1893), Chicago (1892) and Lowell, Massachusetts (1904). It was the brothers Stephano in 1900 who first envisioned the gathering of a Greek Orthodox parish in the tristate area. They instituted a tithing system for the early immigrants arriving here with the purpose of establishing a parish. Employees of the Stephano tobacco business were the first to enroll, and the descendants of these first families are still with the Church of the Annunciation in Elkins Park.

Philadelphia's Church of the Annunciation was founded in 1901. Until a permanent house of worship was established, its faithful worshiped at various temporary locations, finally acquiring a permanent site on South 12th Street at Fitzwater. This was originally an Episcopal house of worship, purchased from the Episcopal Diocese and subsequently converted into an Orthodox house of worship. It was here that the first Greek Orthodox communicants in the tristate area would worship for the following six decades.

The early priests who served the Church of the Annunciation were missionaries. They traveled great distances between Philadelphia and Washington, Pittsburgh and New York. Interim priests then followed these missionaries to perform the sacraments of the Church, to bury the dead, and to maintain the beginnings of the parochial school system. In 1923 a second parish began to gather in Philadelphia on South 8th Street, soon to be known as St. George's. Many others soon followed throughout the Delaware Valley.

The Church of the Annunciation remained in Philadelphia until the 1960s. However, as a result of the gradual urban deterioration and the subsequent, gradual integration of its congregation into the surrounding suburbs, it became necessary to relocate the physical plant of the parish to Elkins Park. The first location was on Elkins Avenue, and a few years later, five acres on the corner of Old York Road and Elkins Avenue were purchased. During this period the pastor of the parish was the Very Rev. Neophytos Spyroglannakis, the former archdeacon of the late Archbishop Michael, primate of the Church in America, now stationed in Toronto.

Many pastors have led the Annunciation parish. Father Thomas Daniel was succeeded by Fr. John Kyriazis, who served as pastor until 1925 and who was followed by Frs. Constantine Papanicolou, John Danaskos, Constantine Hatzidemetriou, John Gerotheou and Aimilianos Lalousis, taking us to 1935. They were succeeded by Joachim Isidorides and George Papademetriou up to 1968 and then by Paul Economides. Fr. John A. Limberakis succeeded Fr. Economides in 1970 and is the current pastor of Annunciation. Fr. Limberakis is the first American born (Boston) priest to serve the parish.

Since 1970 the parish has acquired a new Byzantine style religious/cultural complex with a beautiful church edifice. The opening (Thyranoxia) ceremonies were conducted on November 19, 1972 by Archbishop Iakovos, Primate of the church in America. The entire complex was designed by Demetrios Siderakis of New York City and erected by the local firm, Luckens Construction Co. of North Wales.

The religious artifacts of the church are authentic Byzantine appointments designed and manufactured in Athens. Its iconography is genuinely Byzantine, created by George Filippakis of New York City and the late George N. Gleatas of Athens. The white marble Holy Table (Altar) as well as the Corinthian columns which stand in the nave and in the exterior portals of the edifice were all hewn by the Efstratios Filippotis firm in Athens.

The Greek Orthodox Church is a worldwide fellowship of believers united in the faith. It flowers on every continent, cuts across all races, follows its people in languages and cultures identified with all the peoples of the earth. It was among the founding members of the World Council of Churches (1948) and participates in the National Council of Churches. It is among the most committed churches presently involved in the ecumenical movement.

Little did those early immigrants at the turn of the century realize what rapid growth their church would experience here and throughout the land. In but half a century the original five or six parishes in America grew in excess of a hundred-fold. Of all the parishes of the Greek Orthodox Archdiocese in the Americas, a judicatory of the Ecumenical Patriarchate of Constantinople in Istanbul, Elkins Park's Annunciation parish is among the oldest. In the tristate region it is the mother parish, the parent of parishes in Philadelphia and Upper Darby, thence to Wilmington, Chester (now Media), Broomall and Cherry Hill, Norristown and beyond.

Many groups meet in the Church of the Annunciation to learn from its rich imagery the customs of the Greek heritage. One is the Philoptochos Society, a culturally oriented group, formed to transmit customs from one generation to another. Others are PTO, YAL, and JOY, each embracing a segment of the parish. The church also supports charities that enhance the local and national programs of the church. Annunciation/Evangelismos brings together the continuation of traditional worship, the preservation of culture, and an ongoing sense of commitment to community.

*"Jesus and Mary, apostles and saints, the very
foundations of faith surround the worshipper and light up the church …"*

Church of the Annunciation

TOUR

The arched colonnade and the glittering dome of the church pull the visitor into a Byzantine world that becomes even more real once you enter the narthex. This church reflects centuries of tradition where patterns of worship have evolved since the time of Christ and where patterns of architecture are rooted in the Justinian period. All church appointments follow strict rules of appearance and form.

In the narthex itself, the ceremony of the church first becomes apparent. Long white candles are lit by worshippers, who join Christ in shedding light on the world. In front of you and to the right are the first of the icons that adorn the church within. Icons are flat images, produced in two-dimensional form upon wood, canvas, plaster, or with mosaics. Icons are windows that open heavenward. They are the teaching vehicles for those whose literacy is limited, according to Orthodox teachings. Consecrated, they become sacred art that is venerated. Here, the icons represent the archetype of the original biblical personage or scene. The congregation emotionally identifies with these images that the church recognizes as part of the incarnation.

From left to right, facing the entrance, the icons represent: St. Panteleimon, the eleventh-century physician and miracle worker, Christ, and the Annunciation of the Blessed Virgin Mary to whose honor the church is dedicated. To the right, above the candle box, is the Icon of the Dormition of Mary, marking the death or falling asleep in the Lord of Mary.

Walk through the doors to the beauty of the Byzantine tradition. Your first impression might be the sense of dimension and depth that is produced by the use of light and color. Columns mark the length of the nave and a rounded dome soars above clerestory windows. Throughout there is the use of brilliant color taken directly from nature without the mixing of the hues, characteristic of eleventh-century style. Notice the alternating use of red and green brick and the repeated colors of the far niches next to the sanctuary. The marble columns that are crowned with Corinthian capitals are separated by arches painted in a light turquoise. This color is repeated and deepened right below the dome and in the apse itself. The eye is drawn powerfully towards the sanctuary.

Unlike some of the other Old York Road churches and synagogues, creative effort has not been put into stained glass, as anthropomorphic images in stained glass are not traditional in the Greek Orthodox Church. The windows here merely let in light, but they do contain circles that are repeated in all the windows of the church, in those of the dome and above the doors, and in the shapes carved into the doors themselves. The light rays take on the hue of the stained glass, some gold, some blue. The archways and the niches next to the sanctuary repeat this circular form. Along the simple walls, the windows separate icons that are almost as large as the windows themselves. The north wall supports icons of saints of the female gender; on the south wall hang icons of saints of the male gender.

All of these holy personages are easily identifiable to the churchgoer, for the form of representation does not differ from church to church or from artist to artist. Produced by priests and nuns as well as lay experts, the icons do not list the names of the individual artists who painted them. Their identities are not as important as are the subjects of the paintings. What is essential is that the icons follow the prescribed pattern of design that makes all Byzantine art seem familiar. The figures seem related by form, by the austere, ascetic and elongated faces with the curved brows and large, dilated eyes, and by the use of

Icon of the Transfiguration.

prophetic symbol (*Ezekiel* 1:10); a lion, an ox, a face of a human, and an eagle, respectively. There are plans to complete the dome by painting the icon of Christ in the dome's center, to be known as the *Pantocrator* (Sovereign God Almighty). The images of prophets will be placed between the windows, and a vine, symbolic of Christ's relationship to his followers, will flow beneath the windows around the dome's belt.

Within the north transept, to the left, is the marble baptismal font, carved in 1901 in Athens. Behind the font is a carved screen that shows the Baptism of Christ. On either side of the Baptism scene is the Lord's Prayer and the Creed both in Greek and in English translation, appearing in symmetric panels.

To the left of the font is the symbol of the Holy Sepulchre, where Christ was buried. It is carved from olive wood and then gold-leafed. Four intricately designed angels form the side posts which support the canopy that rises above them. Below the canopy rests

specific colors. Abundant use of gold leaf as the background color allows the icons to light up the dark walls. Vigil lamps hang before each of the icons elsewhere.

Next to each saint are smaller icons that portray major events in the lives of Christ and Mary. Along the north wall the scenes move counter-clockwise, beginning with the Presentation of Mary and proceeding to the Transfiguration. Here Moses and Elijah, Old Testament prophets, stand with Peter, John and James, the disciples. The Old Testament is considered to be as sacred as the New, as an essential precursor to the latter. Along the south wall, the scenes move clockwise from the Crucifixion to the final scene of the Pentecost.

Walk towards the transept of the church. At the base of the dome the four Evangelists, who recorded the life of Jesus, are painted on the pendentives. In clockwise order starting over the pulpit are: Mark, Luke, Matthew, and John, each represented by his

Representation of the Holy Sepulchre in gold-leafed olive wood.

gold brocaded velvet that tells of the burial of Christ. Notice the use of icons here as well, as Mary, John, and an archangel surround the body of Christ entombed.

In front of the sanctuary is the Iconostasis, a screen of icons that sets apart the solea (chancel) from the rest of the church. Here icons represent, from left to right, the Archangel Michael, the Annunciation, and Mary and the Christ Child. The latter forms a warm image of maternal love as Mary embraces the Child lovingly in her bosom. Their faces are on the same level. This icon is known as the *Glykophilousa*, the sweet kissing. Jesus wraps his arms around his mother, looking at her, as Mary gazes outward into the congregation. The icons continue with Christ, St. John the Baptist, shown here with the traditional wings behind him, and the Archangel Gabriel.

Look through the gates of the Iconstasis to the altar (holy table) within the sanctuary. The altar stands on four columns that symbolize the four evangelists, and the square column in the center represents the head of Christ. Thus the altar is the foundation on which is celebrated the liturgy. It is also symbolic of the table in the Upper Room in Jerusalem where Christ and his disciples gathered for the Last Supper.

On the wall of the apse rising behind the altar, Mary stands but seems as light as the soaring angels on either side of her. At her feet are the symbols of humanity in the form of Adam and Eve who venerate Mary and Jesus. In the walls of the apse are two niches that hold icons of Christ. To the left is his Holy Nativity and to the right is the traditional symbol for the Resurrection. Here Christ descends to Hades, raising the hands of Adam and Eve as he promises to raise all humanity. Around him are the kings of the Old Testament, Solomon and David, who appear with St. John. Christ is standing on the Gates of Hell that have fallen to form a cross. The sanctuary is vibrant in its blues and roses, highlighted by gold leaf.

Above the north and south transept doors are more icons that venerate holy personages. But there is an icon of St. John in the south transept, to the left of the door, that is particularly interesting. As the winged messenger-prophet, who foretold the coming of Christ, he stands in a surreal landscape. In his hands, he holds his own severed head. Behind him, the executioner's axe leans against a barren tree. The icon celebrates the two feast days (January 7th and August 29th) linked to the Saint, rather than depicting the Saint's knowledge of his own death. But to the viewer who is aware of the Biblical story, the icon takes on chilling meaning.

Many Biblical lessons, following Byzantine tradition, dot the walls of this church in their linear beauty. Jesus and Mary, apostles and saints, the very foundations of faith surround the worshipper and light up the walls of the church with their bold colors and gold leaf.

Iconostasis with Mary and the Christ Child.

Beth Sholom Congregation

Beth Sholom Congregation
Old York Road and Foxcroft Road, Elkins Park

HISTORY

In its history, Beth Sholom Congregation has had two rabbis; Rabbi Mortimer J. Cohen served the congregation from 1919 to 1964 and Rabbi Aaron Landes from 1964 until the present.

Rabbi Mortimer J. Cohen came to a newly organized congregation in the Logan section of Philadelphia and met the challenge of forging a small group of inexperienced synagogue lay leaders into a significant American Jewish congregation within the Conservative Movement. Under his leadership the congregation survived the pressures of the Depression and the rigors of World War II.

Rabbi Cohen was a man of remarkable vision. He organized a strong Men's Club and Sisterhood. He helped to develop a Religious School. He presided at the building of the synagogue in Logan. Following World War II, Rabbi Cohen saw the movement of married children of his congregants to the northern suburbs and determined that Beth Sholom had to follow these younger families. He prevailed upon his leadership to purchase land in Elkins Park so that Beth Sholom would become the first congregation in the City of Philadelphia to move to the suburbs following World War II.

Beth Sholom Center in Elkins Park, with its facilities for catering, swimming pool, Fischman Memorial Auditorium-Gymnasium, Sheerr Religious School Building and Price Chapel, was completed and dedicated in 1952. In 1966, the Samuel and Anna Cross Annex to the Sheerr Religious School was built. Services were held, alternately, in the Logan synagogue and at the Center. With the growth of the congregation in the suburbs, the Board of Directors decided that a new synagogue building should be added to the Elkins Park Center and that it should be one that would capture the imagination of the Jewish community.

It was at this point that the services of the internationally famed architect, Frank Lloyd Wright, were obtained. An easy fellowship developed between Wright and Rabbi Cohen, and the architectural landmark that resulted from this collaboration is, of course, described in detail in the article that follows. Rabbi Cohen continued to lead Beth Sholom until 1964 when he retired as Rabbi Emeritus. He was active in the life of the synagogue until his death in 1972.

The second era in the brief history of Beth Sholom Congregation began in 1964 when Rabbi Aaron Landes was invited to succeed Rabbi Cohen by the president of the congregation, Edward Taxin. Taxin also played a significant role in the congregation's transition between the eras presided over by Rabbi Cohen and Rabbi Landes.

Following his ordination from Jewish Theological Seminary in New York, Rabbi Landes served two years on active duty with the United States Navy. During that tour he was instrumental in the founding of the first synagogue in the history of the United States Navy, the Uriah P. Levy Chapel in Norfolk, Virginia. During all of the years of Rabbi Landes' rabbinic service, he has maintained another career as a Chaplain in the United States Naval Reserve. He was at retirement in 1989 the highest ranking Naval Reserve Chaplain in the United States of America with the rank of Rear Admiral. Rabbi Landes is also a past National Chaplain of the Naval Reserve Association and is the only rabbi ever to have served in that capacity. He is currently National Chaplain of the Jewish War Veterans of the United States and Chairman of the National JWB, Jewish Chaplains Council, which endorses rabbis for service in the Army, Navy and Air Force.

Rabbi Landes heads a fine staff at Beth Sholom.

The professionals include: Hazzan David F. Tilman, Cantor and Music Director of the congregation; Jacob B. Lieberman, Ritual Director and supervisor of the Bar/Bat Mitzvah program; Sheila Goldstein, Educational Director of Beth Sholom Religious Schools; Mimi Krassenstein, Director of Group Services; and Fred D. Levine, Executive Director. With a gifted staff as a major source of strength, programming at Beth Sholom expanded into many new areas.

When he came to Beth Sholom Congregation in 1964, Rabbi Landes found that, like other suburban congregations, Beth Sholom could not get a daily *Minyan* (religious quorum of ten worshipers) on a regular basis in the morning and in the evening. His style was to lead by personal example. He began to attend the morning and evening Minyan on a daily basis. With the active support of lay leaders, within three years 40 to 60 people were coming every morning. Beth Sholom continues to attract several dozen people every morning of the year at its early service and has a *Minyan* every evening also.

Beth Sholom also prides itself on the success of its educational program. The national average of children who continue in Jewish education following Bar and Bat Mitzvah in the United States in about twelve percent. Beth Sholom, in 1964, was no different. Rabbi Landes marshalled the congregation's forces to raise the standards of the Beth Sholom Religious School, both in the elementary and the high school levels. Using the enthusiasm of Bar and Bat Mitzvah preparation, he secured commitments from children and parents to continue in the Hebrew High School Program.

The Conservative Movement supports a summer camp called Camp Ramah, which provides a total traditional Jewish living experience for all of its campers. Beth Sholom strongly encourages its students to attend Camp Ramah, with the result that the largest delegation of students from any greater Philadelphia congregation at Ramah comes from its student body. A number of scholarships were established to help in motivating children and families to receive this enriching total religious experience over the summer.

Beth Sholom was one of the first congregations in Philadelphia to engage a full-time Youth Director. The youth congregation of Beth Sholom has become an important supplement to the Religious Educational Program, over and above the hours that the children spend in their formal religious school studies. Through the youth congregation, many of the religious practices learned in formal study become living experiences on Sabbaths and holidays.

With a Cantor possessing a Masters Degree in Choral Conducting from Juilliard, Beth Sholom was able to develop excellent musical programs. Hazzan Tilman trains a children's chorus of 60 voices and an adult chorus of 50 voices. Both choruses have achieved city wide and national reputations. The congregation celebrates music festivals with both choruses and an orchestra within the congregation. Each of the choruses is invited to sing in the greater Philadelphia area. They have participated in concerts at Lincoln Center in New York as well as in Israel.

Due to neighborhood population shifts, the West Oak Lane Jewish Community Center voted in 1978 to merge with Beth Sholom. They brought with them a number of Torah Scrolls which they and Beth Sholom then gave as gifts to new and struggling congregations in suburban Philadelphia, New Jersey and Israel.

When Rabbi Landes came to the congregation in 1964, the congregation had grown from the approximately 400 families who had been affiliated in Logan to about 900 in Elkins Park. In recent years, though there was little new home construction in the immediate area, Beth Sholom has continued to grow. It now has a membership in excess of 1300 families. The Young Marrieds membership is the fastest growing element within the congregation, and the average age within the synagogue is decreasing.

In the early '70s, Rabbi Landes saw the need for an Elementary Hebrew Day School in the northern suburbs. The Solomon Schechter School was meeting at Congregation Har Zion in the west, and children from the northeast and the northern suburbs found the travel too burdensome. Rabbi Landes approached the children of the late Max and Sadie Forman and broached the idea of a Day School to them as a living memorial to their parents. The family was enthusiastic about the idea and donated an initial gift to Beth Sholom for the sole purpose of opening a Day School. In September 1973, the Day School opened with a kindergarten of twenty children, under the principalship of Sora E. Landes; it has grown into a school with an enrollment of 140 children. The Forman Hebrew Day School developed a reputation for excellence in its general studies and Hebrew studies and met at Beth Sholom Congregation for thirteen years. It is now a part of the educational complex at the Mandell Campus, located on York Road between St. John's Lutheran Church and Congregation Adath Jeshurun.

Beth Sholom Congregation, now in its seventy-first year, is a leading Conservative Congregation in the United States of America. Throughout its history, Beth Sholom Congregation has been a pioneer and innovator. It is truly "a House of Prayer for all people."

The theme of Frank Lloyd Wright's
synagogue is Mount Sinai resting in the hands of God.

Beth Sholom Congregation

TOUR

Well before 1953 Rabbi Mortimer J. Cohen understood the need for a place of worship for his congregation in the growing northern suburbs of Philadelphia. But it was not until 1953 that the Rabbi entered into a three-year exchange with the world-renowned architect, Frank Lloyd Wright.

Rabbi Cohen envisioned a modern synagogue that would reflect the ideals of Judaism and the best of the American tradition, a synagogue that would represent and evolve from the elements of Jewish faith. Rabbi Cohen began by making sketches of his vision. He contacted Boris Blai, who was then Dean of Temple's Tyler School of Art. Blai quickly recommended Wright, then finishing the Guggenheim Museum in New York, as the architect who could share Rabbi Cohen's vision. Wright, the son of a Presbyterian Minister and a practicing Unitarian, was well informed about the laws, history and details of the Jewish religion. An easy fellowship developed between the two men, one that allowed the architect to work closely with the Rabbi in planning every aspect, every nuance of the synagogue's design.

Much of Wright's architecture has sculpturesque qualities, forming masses that utilize modern materials that are shaped only after the needs, or function, of the building are well understood. Ornamentation grows out of the materials employed. Wright was open to the possibilities of any given situation as he approached each new assignment. Beth Sholom would be different from his other buildings, and it would also be the last architectural project before his death in 1959.

An aerial view of the synagogue would make the building's hexagonal shape immediately apparent. Wright would explain the choice of shape by cupping his two hands together with the palms up and the thumbs held closely to the sides. When worshippers entered the synagogue, he believed, they were held in the hands of God. The shape formed by the cupped hands is a hexagon. The glass dome that juts from the center of the building represents Mount Sinai where Judaism states Moses received the tablets of the Law, or the Ten Commandments, from God. Thus the theme of the building is Mount Sinai resting in the hands of God. As Moses received the law under a sky filled with fire and lightning, Wright illuminated the dome at night, making the structure a flaming Mount Sinai resting still in the hands of God.

View the building from the front entrance and notice two concrete extensions that extend from the left and right sides. Here are representations of the thumbs of God, as Wright completed his image in each detail. In front of the entrance is a fountain that reflects an ancient tradition. The Laver, made of copper in the ancient Temple, offered the worshipper an opportunity to cleanse or purify himself before engaging in prayer. Here the flowing waters of the fountain recall this practice. Directly over the front entrance is a canopy that projects forward over the heads of the entering congregation. Like the hands of the ancient priest held over the heads of his congregation in benediction, the canopy reminds the worshipper of the continuity of the Jewish faith.

Wright employed modern materials in his building. Concrete, steel, aluminum, glass, and corrugated plastic are fashioned together to build this mountain. Two of the three steel beams that support the dome are easily visible from the front entrance. They are 116 feet long and weight 110 tons, and represent the three Patriarchs of the Jewish faith: Abraham, Isaac and Jacob. The menorah, often seen in front of other synagogues, has been incorporated into the exterior design itself. Seven flames jut upward from each of the steel spines and are, like the dome itself, illumi-

Steps to Main Sanctuary.

Soaring elevation of Main Sanctuary.

nated at night. The worshipper is reminded once again that God created the world in six days, and on the seventh, He rested.

All the details in the synagogue's interior were carefully chosen by Wright to further the theme of the building. Stand in the foyer and notice the steps on the left and the right that lead up to the main Sanctuary and the steps that lead downstairs to the Sisterhood Chapel. Climb the gentle slope of the steps to the Main Sanctuary, moving upward past a concrete dividing wall to the light-filled room. Entering the Sanctuary, the visitor immediately senses the openness of the area, the height of the towering dome overhead and the wash of light that enters through the layers of glass and corrugated plastic. Etched steel bands separate the sheets of translucent material. Before you is the sweep of seats that allows seating for over a thousand people.

The repeated triangular forms are obvious. Tri-

angles are in the clustering of the seating, grouped so worshippers can view the person on the other side of the room since all there are part of *K'lal Yisrael*, one community of Israel praying together. Interlocking triangles that form the Star of David are the lights covering the ceilings in the multi-leveled building. Triangles house the heating and air conditioning ducts. Triangles puncture the wood of the lecterns, reader's desk, and the Ark itself on the *Bima*.

True to his fashion, Wright designed all the elements in the synagogue, including the furniture. Even the colors are part of the overall concept of the synagogue. The carpet is symbolic of the desert sand beneath the Hebrews who wandered for forty years before receiving the Law. The terra cotta of the chairs is like the desert sand reflecting the sun's light; the grey metal used for the chair frames is like the iron ore that exists in the sand as well.

Walk towards the *Bima*, noticing the inward slope

Bima and Ark of Main Sanctuary.

of the floor as Wright meant to suggest the cupped palms of God's hands. The floor's slope also draws the worshipper inward towards the holy Ark and suggests the words in Psalm 130: "*Out of the depths have I called to Thee, O Lord.*"

Color in the Sanctuary hovers around the Ark and is present in the enormous chandelier that hangs in the center of the dome. Beside the wooden Ark, massive cement monoliths rise to forty feet, suggesting the stone tables given to Moses. The Ark doors reveal a gold curtain that suggests the light of the Torah radiating outward to all. Inside are ten Torah scrolls that remind the worshipper of God's commandments.

Above the Ark, the *Ner Tamid* shines eternally. Wright and Rabbi Cohen reached into the Book of Isaiah for the design of the light. As a young man, the prophet had a vision of God in the Temple. Here God was surrounded by Seraphim and Cherubim who sang:

Kadosh, kadosh, kadosh Adonai Tz'vaot
melo chol haarets k'vodo.
Holy, holy, holy is the Lord of Hosts,
the Earth is filled with His glory.

The red flame is nestled here, burning among gold angel wings. The six arches on either side of the Ark are symbolic of the six books of *Mishna*, the classic rabbinic interpretation of the Law. On top of each arch is a straight pole with five round bulbs projecting outward, representing the five Books of Moses.

Dropping eighty-nine feet from the center of the eleven story dome, the chandelier repeats the triangular motif in brilliant color. This too was designed with an element of Judaism in mind. Jewish mysticism taught that God reveals himself to mankind by the emanation of colored light. Blue reflects wisdom, red represents strength, yellow is beauty, green means understanding, and white symbolizes mercy or loving kindness. The mystics believed that the original twelve tribes of Israel understood God's colors. Therefore Wright added twelve white lights that project from the sides of the chandelier.

When Wright was asked why he allowed the walls of the dome to remain undecorated, he answered that God would be the master painter. God, Wright felt, would add the golden color of the sun or would reflect a muted cloudy sky by adding silver. When asked about the cracking sounds the dome seems to emit, Wright answered that the expansion and contraction of the materials made the building a living organism.

While this Main Sanctuary is obviously the focal point of the synagogue, other buildings complete the complex and allow space for Beth Sholom's many activities. The original Beth Sholom Center, now the

Bima and Ark of Sisterhood Chapel.

Philip L. Sheerr Religious School Building, holds classes for both adults and youngsters. The Samuel and Anna Cross Annex houses the library and offices.

Beth Sholom members offer detailed tours of the Wright building. Visitors have come from all over the world to view Wright's creation, noting the small, red signature plaque that hangs, as on all Wright's buildings, near the front entrance. Visitors are struck by the dramatic simplicity of Wright's and Rabbi Cohen's vision, by the power of the towering dome, and by repeated themes that unify the decorative elements.

However, members are quick to remind the visitor, Beth Sholom is more than just a building. Those who attend Beth Sholom are equally proud of the spirit within. They extend the family spirit they feel to all visitors, to those who enter as strangers but who leave as friends.

Reform Congregation Keneseth Israel

Reform Congregation Keneseth Israel

Old York Road and Township Line, Elkins Park

HISTORY

Keneseth Israel, "Assembly of Israel," was founded in 1847. It was the fourth congregation to be established by the expanding Jewish community of Philadelphia. Its official language for religious services and business was German, and that pattern remained unchanged for forty years or until the arrival of Dr. Joseph Krauskopf, K.I.'s third Senior Rabbi.

Orthodox in observance at first, Keneseth Israel adopted Reform in 1855, and thus became the first progressive congregation in Philadelphia and only the fifth in the entire country to take the way of radical experimentation. For almost forty years, Keneseth Israel was the only Reform congregation in Philadelphia.

For the first fourteen years of its existence, the temple had no rabbi but retained a series of "readers" to conduct services. Physically the congregation was first located at 528 N. 2nd Street in Philadelphia; it moved successively to New Market and Noble Streets (1853), 6th and Brown Streets (1863), 1717 N. Broad Street (1892), and York Road and Township Line, Elkins Park, (1957). Each move was prompted by the need for larger and more modern facilities to serve an ever-expanding constituency.

The first Senior Rabbi to serve the congregation was Dr. David Einhorn, one of the founders of Reform Judaism, who came to K.I. in 1861. Einhorn literally had to flee from his pulpit in Baltimore, where his outspoken opposition to slavery had made it unsafe for him to remain. He was followed by Dr. Samuel Hirsch, formerly Chief Rabbi of Luxembourg, in 1866. Hirsch served K.I. for twenty years, moving K.I. toward more radical reform. Hirsch played a leading role in the formulation of the "Pittsburgh Platform" of 1885 which clearly delineated Reform Judaism's break with traditional beliefs and practices and set standards for the movement which lasted more than half

a century.

1887 marked the beginning of the illustrious thirty-six-year stewardship of Dr. Joseph Krauskopf, the congregation's first English-speaking rabbi. In those thirty-six years, Dr. Krauskopf wrote his own prayer book, established a worship format which included Friday evening services and Sunday morning services at which his lectures on a variety of current subjects drew large crowds. Under his leadership Keneseth Israel became the largest Jewish congregation in North America.

After a trip to Russia in 1894 where he met with Leo Tolstoi and observed at first hand the squalor and persecution of Russian Jewry, Krauskopf conceived the idea of a school to train young Jewish immigrants as farmers. That school, originally the National Farm School, now Delaware Valley College of Science and Agriculture in Doylestown, was the setting for K.I.'s congregational picnics for many years. Krauskopf was one of America's leading rabbis and was elected to the presidency of the Central Conference of American Rabbis in 1903.

Dr. William H. Fineshriber succeeded Dr. Krauskopf and served K.I. with distinction for twenty-five years, from 1924-1949. A brilliant speaker, he raised the Sunday morning lectures to new heights of popularity which ended only when repairs to the Temple dome caused that format to be abandoned. He brought back some of the practices discarded by his predecessors, including Bar Mitzvah and the reading of the Torah on Saturday mornings, and introduced the then-new Union Prayer Book to the congregation. Politically, Dr. Fineshriber was an anti-Zionist, casting his lot with the American Council for Judaism, although his feelings in that area began to change shortly before his death.

The congregation moved in new, different and

challenging directions under the dynamic leadership of Dr. Bertram W. Korn, the first K.I. product to become its rabbi. During his thirty years as Senior Rabbi, Dr. Korn brought many changes to the congregation. The late Friday evening service became the centerpiece of the worship structure. The Religious School, aided by the post-war baby boom, mushroomed into a system requiring three shifts, one on Saturday and two on Sunday. The congregation changed from its anti-Zionist stance and became openly supportive of Israel. K.I.'s move to the present location in Elkins Park in 1957 aided and abetted much of the change and growth. Dr. Korn became the first Jewish Chaplain to achieve star rank in any of the services — Rear Admiral in the U.S. Naval Reserve — and his excellence as a preacher perpetuated the high pulpit standards established by his predecessors.

Rabbi Simeon J. Maslin was elected the sixth Senior Rabbi of Keneseth Israel in 1980, shortly after the death of Dr. Korn. Rabbi Maslin is the author of numerous articles and two volumes on Jewish practices, and he continues K.I.'s tradition of dynamic pulpit oratory. He attempts to maintain the traditional Jewish tension between the universalistic and the particular, stressing at the same time the responsibility of the Jewish community for the welfare of all people and the need to assure Jewish survival through the practice of *mitzvot* — Jewish rituals — and the study of Torah. Rabbi Maslin is currently the president of the Board of Rabbis of Greater Philadelphia, and he serves on the national boards of several major Jewish organizations.

One of K.I.'s most innovative programs of community service was instituted in 1984. Through the generosity of anonymous members, K.I. has been able to "challenge" area churches and synagogues to make gifts of $500 or more to shelters for the homeless and to soup kitchens around Christmas/Chanukah time. Each gift of $500 is matched by K.I. so that participating congregations can send $1000 to the shelters of their choice. This program, now in its sixth year, results in donations of over $40,000 each year to twenty-five or more shelters. Most of the churches and synagogues included in this book participate in K.I.'s "Matching Grants for the Homeless" program.

Among other major programs instituted at K.I. in recent years is the annual music service dedicated to the memory of Rabbi Bertram W. Korn. The Korn Memorial Fund commissions a major Jewish composer to compose a new setting for some part of the liturgy each year and to premiere the composition at a Sabbath service. Through the publication of these new compositions, the musical repertoire of synagogues all over North America has been enriched.

Other new programs include the annual Conference on Grief, for which the entire community is invited to spend an afternoon at K.I. to hear a prominent authority on the process of grief and healing, followed by seminars led by grief therapists. The K.I. Sisterhood sponsors the very successful annual Cheltenham Antiques Fair and conducts an annual Interfaith Service which usually attracts several hundred women. The K.I. Brotherhood offers a series of Sunday brunches with guest lecturers. And the "Sharing is Caring" Committee provides food, clothing, friendly visits and other services to the lonely elderly.

In addition to Rabbi Maslin, Keneseth Israel has an Associate Rabbi/Director of Education, Joel Alpert; an Assistant Rabbi, Shoshana Perry; a Cantor, Richard Allen; a Temple Administrator, William Ferstenfeld, who currently serves as president of the National Association of Temple Administrators; an Organist/Choir Director, Sharon Bertha MacCabe; a secretarial staff and a Religious School faculty. Services are held every Friday evening and Saturday morning through the year, and a large Nursery School and Religious School function effectively through the school year. K.I.'s rabbis are ably assisted in the leading of services by a corps of lay readers, and members of the congregation serve in the leadership of virtually every major social service organization and philanthropy in the Delaware Valley.

The Congregation still holds to the goals of its founders: to maintain a synagogue as a center of worship, religious education and communal gathering; to foster a "living Judaism" not only in the synagogue, but also in the homes and lives of its members and their families; and to adjust the teachings and practices of old to the needs of each new generation of American Jews. Rich in years and distinguished in history, Keneseth Israel, one of America's largest congregations, maintains its dedication to the creative survival of Judaism as an eternal "light to the nations."

*On the pulpit the muted tones of marble
and wood; in the windows the bold message of the prophets.*

Reform Congregation Keneseth Israel

TOUR

While the main entrance to Keneseth Israel is on York Road, just south of Township Line, most people use the parking lot entrance. Here they are welcomed by a sculpture of the family, two parents clasping arms to encircle the children between them. Given by the Binswanger family and designed by Joseph Greenberg, Jr., the sculpture faces the synagogue as if to indicate one of the cornerstones of Judaism: the family and its faith.

The large building that houses Congregation Keneseth Israel today was dedicated in 1957, after 110 years in the City of Philadelphia. It is a multi-purpose building with a three-story school wing of thirty attractive classrooms and several offices; the Krauskopf Auditorium; the Meyers Library (possibly the largest synagogue library in the Delaware Valley), on the second floor above the entrance; a second social hall, Rothschild Auditorium, at the far end of the school wing; an office for Kosher Meals-on-Wheels that provides daily meals for elderly shut-ins; a Judaica gift shop; and, on the lower level adjacent to the Rudolph Nursery School classrooms, the Youth Canteen. Outside the Nursery classrooms is a well-equipped nursery playground. Virtually unnoticed in a secondary York Road entrance foyer is a Tiffany-style window, a remnant of the former synagogue on Broad Street.

Just to the left of the parking lot entrance is a lead and stained glass illuminated mural with the legend: *"Come, let us go into the House of the Lord."* Passing through the glass doors, one enters a spacious marble lobby dedicated to the memory of K.I.'s fourth Senior Rabbi, William Fineshriber. To the left hang the portraits of the five senior Rabbis who led the congregation between 1860 and 1979. Farthest on the right is Dr. David Einhorn who, because of his radical abolitionist views, was forced to flee from Baltimore in 1861. Then there are Drs. Samuel Hirsch, Joseph Krauskopf, William Fineshriber and Bertram Korn.

Directly ahead are windows that were taken from the North Broad St. synagogue when the congregation moved to Elkins Park. The center panel depicts Ruth and Naomi on the left and Abraham and Isaac on the right. These windows are very different in style from the modern windows in the Chapel and Main Sanctuary but have been retained to recall the roots of the congregation. On the left is a window that was dedicated to Theodore Roosevelt. He was honored for his role in influencing the Russian government to moderate the persecution of the Jews at the turn of the century.

Off the right side of the foyer is the Temple Judea Museum of Keneseth Israel, which contains one of the finest collections of Judaica in the Northeast. The Museum is a memorial to Temple Judea, a congregation that joined Keneseth Israel in 1982. Both Keneseth Israel and Temple Judea had impressive collections of Jewish ceremonial objects, Temple Judea's having been collected over many years by Emeritus Rabbi Meir Lasker. The proper memorial for Temple Judea was obvious, and so today the Temple Judea Museum adorns the lobby with a continually changing series of exhibits from a rich collection of Jewish art and artifacts.

The Museum is especially proud to own the second oldest marriage contract or *ketubah*, in America, dated 1778. When the Museum was being planned, Rabbi Maslin remembered a tradition preserved by the Great Synagogue of Rome. Set within the walls of that Sanctuary are the Arks preserved from abandoned and destroyed Italian synagogues. And so today, on the right wall of the Temple Judea Museum, is the Ark from the former Temple Judea building. Now the classical columns of the Ark form a frame for several

Temple Judea Museum in Fineshriber Lobby.

exhibition shelves, and former members of Temple Judea can see the Ark before which they once prayed.

Hanging in front of the Ark is a beautiful Italian *Ner Tamid*, dedicated in 1833 to the memory of an aristocratic Italian-Jewish family, the Ottolenghis. The Museum also possesses a precious book from the sixteenth century, a commentary of the Torah. This book, as an inscription attests, was originally in possession of the same Ottolenghi family. Within this Museum, then, two historic artifacts of the ancient Italian Jewish community are brought together.

Through doors to the left of the lobby is the Neumann Chapel which offers an intimate atmosphere in which to worship. Simply appointed, the Ark is the focal point, as in all synagogues. Above are the tablets depicting the Ten Commandments and the ever-radiant Eternal Light. The walls of the Chapel are covered with brass plaques, memorializing the names of the dead. When the *Yahrzeit* (anniversary of death) occurs, the names are illuminated by small bulbs.

Along the outside wall are five stained glass windows, designed by the Rambusch Studio of New York in 1960, representing, from left to right, Moses, Isaiah,

Esther, Hillel and a fascinating bit of Americana. This fifth window depicts Robert Morris, Pennsylvania signer of the Declaration of Independence, clasping the hand of Haym Salomon, the Jewish financier who backed the Revolutionary War. Morris reaches out to Salomon's shoulder, as if to enclose him in an embrace of respect and camaraderie. Both men are dressed in colonial garb and stand in front of Independence Hall.

The slogan on this window is the verse from Leviticus, Chapter 25, that is engraved on the Liberty Bell: "*Proclaim liberty throughout the land and unto all the inhabitants thereof.*" The *shofar*, or ram's horn, used to proclaim the New Year in the Jewish tradition, rests at the bottom. Above the figures are bold symbols of America: the eagle holds the Liberty Bell, tilted as it rings out, and behind, the American flag waves. These symbols are as dominant as the two figures of the men beneath and are emblazoned in the glass by the brilliant colors. These chapel windows represent the bold sweep of Jewish history. Beginning with Bible figures to the left, the final window links ancient Jewish history with the modern American Jewish community, as represented by Philadelphia patriot,

Neumann Chapel with Ark and windows depicting Moses, Isaiah and Queen Esther.

Haym Salomon.

In contrast to the intimacy of the Chapel, the Main Sanctuary, reached through doors to the right of the Fineshriber Lobby, seats 850 in its usual configuration and can be expanded, through the removal of the rear wall, to accommodate 2200 worshippers. Elevated by a series of steps, the Ark is the focal point. Set into marble, it is surrounded by the rich texture of the stone. On either side of the Ark doors are brass-color reliefs depicting details from the life of Moses, beginning with Pharaoh's daughter finding the infant Moses

Ark in Main Sanctuary with reliefs depicting life of Moses.

and ending with Moses' ordaining Joshua before his death.

The use of reliefs continues in the smaller panels set into the grid of the blue wall above and behind the Ark. Repeated randomly, each carving symbolizes some theme of Judaism. There are hands extended in the priestly benediction, Noah's Ark, and the Burning Bush. Holidays are depicted with the *shofar* for Rosh Hashanah, the scales for Yom Kippur (the Day of Judgment), and the candles for Sabbath. The twelve tribes of Israel are also represented through their traditional symbols, as, for example, the Lion of Judah. This blue and brass wall makes a dramatic backdrop for the Ark and the massive stone tablets that rise above it. The Commandments are not represented by numbers or written in the Hebrew language of their origin (as in the Chapel); they are spelled out in English so that each worshiper may read them.

Ten large, boldly colored, stained glass windows, designed by artist Jacob Landau and executed by the Willet Studios, combine radiantly to declare their messages, contrasting with the quiet, understated pulpit and Ark. These windows represent the awesome quest of the prophets and patriarchs who sought to understand God's will and to personify it for the People of Israel. They revealed the potential of a people living in the image of God; they foresaw the destruction of Israel and its eventual renewal. Within each window, the prophets' words are recorded in English and Hebrew. The chosen Biblical passages set the theme for each individual window, as the artist represents the biblical vision.

Through vivid pieces of glass, images explode and come together dramatically in each window. The symbols are not easily discovered, and the viewer finds new pieces to fit together in this jigsaw of intense color each time he studies the windows. Within the kaleidoscopic designs, Landau set the prophets' visions into the modern world. As in the Isaiah window, closest to the *bima* in the west wall, the words: *"The wolf shall dwell with the lamb,"* suggests the reunion that the prophet envisioned after the scattering of the people of Israel. Landau couched this message in modern terms by including the flags of nations of the world in the lower section of the window. Isaiah foresaw a time when all nations would blend into one united world at peace.

In these modern, expressionistic windows, then, the ancient biblical prophecies are linked to the ideals and concerns of today. Landau gives relevance to the prophets' visions, fitting together the slivers of brilliant glass to build powerful symbols of faith. To aid in understanding the details of the windows, Keneseth Israel provides a descriptive guide that can be found near each seat in the Main Sanctuary.

Another essential but virtually invisible element in the K.I. Sanctuary is the Phyllis K. Goldsmith Memorial Pipe Organ. Built by Austin Organs in 1961, this organ, one of the largest in the Philadelphia area, has 52 stops, 47 ranks and 2860 pipes. It is set into a very large, fabric-screened area behind and above the Ark. Several of the world's leading organists have performed on the Goldsmith Organ, and, along with various other instrumental ensembles, it has served as the mainstay of an ambitious musical program.

Also barely visible, set high in the upper right corner of the rear wall, is the window of the audio control booth. There the weekly sermons and choir anthems are recorded for re-broadcast each Saturday morning at 11:00 over FM radio station WIBF. These weekly Sabbath service broadcasts and the live broadcasts of the complete High Holy Day services are directed to the shut-in and elderly who cannot attend services.

Wander along the corridors of K.I., and you will find numerous paintings, sculptures and other art objects along the walls. Included are nineteenth-century paintings from Central and Eastern Europe and more modern Israeli and American works. To the right of the entrance foyer and directly to the rear of the Sanctuary is the spacious Krauskopf Auditorium which is used for congregational and community meetings and a variety of life-cycle celebrations. This Auditorium can be divided into smaller meeting spaces and has a fully equipped kitchen and stage.

There is another auditorium, not quite as large as the Krauskopf, at the far end of the school wing. This one, named for K.I. benefactors Charles and Regina Rothschild, also has a kitchen and makes it possible for two large meetings or receptions to take place simultaneously at K.I.

Outside and just beyond the Rothschild Auditorium is the Fineshriber Garden, an enclosed, serene and verdant place for reflection. In the center is the 1891 cornerstone taken from K.I.'s previous home on N. Broad Street, converted now into a planter. Emerging from the garden on the York Road side, one can walk along the length of the school wing to the main entrance.

As indicated above, the main York Road entrance, with its broad sunken patio, is not used as much as the parking lot entrances on the other side of the building. But here we find a bronze shield set into the center of the patio memorializing the groundbreaking in 1954. Around the shield is the inscription *"The place whereon thou standest is holy"* (*Exodus* 3:5). To the right of the entrance, set into the ivy-covered stone wall, is the 1956 cornerstone. Rising from the flagstone patio is a portico of six pillars that supports two massive concrete lintels. The one facing north is inscribed: *"Hear, O Israel, the Lord our God, the Lord is One;"* and the one facing west is inscribed: *"Thou shalt love thy neighbor as thyself."* And that, of course, is the theme of this volume.

The following five houses of worship all in Jenkintown, are not actually situated on Old York Road:

First Church of Christ, Scientist

Abington Friends Meeting

Church of the Immaculate Conception

Jenkintown United Methodist Church and

Salem Baptist Church

These five form a loop around Old York Road near the center of Jenkintown. As the original impetus for this book derived from the Jenkintown Ministerium, these five distinguished churches are included in this volume along with the York Road churches and synagogues.

First Church of Christ, Scientist

First Church of Christ, Scientist

West Avenue and Washington Lane, Jenkintown

HISTORY*

On the evening of May 12, 1933, seven Christian Scientists met to discuss the feasibility of organizing a Christian Science Church in Jenkintown. Jenkintown seemed the logical place for organizing a new Christian Science branch church as it was the largest borough in the vicinity with a rapidly expanding business district and good transportation services. It was therefore with the earnest desire to further the cause of Christian Science that the first meeting was held. On June 16, 1933, it was unanimously voted to organize First Church of Christ, Scientist, Jenkintown.

The need for a place to hold services was effectively met as the first Sunday service and Sunday School were held in Odd Fellows Hall in Jenkintown on the morning of July 9. On September 29, 1933, the church was formally recognized as a branch of The Mother Church, the First Church of Christ, Scientist, Boston, Massachusetts.

From the very first the membership looked forward with hope to having its own edifice, a church home which would manifest the dignity, beauty, peace and spiritual activity of a true "Church." A building fund was established, and the congregation was able to purchase the lot on the corner of Washington Lane and West Avenue where the church now stands.

Plans were submitted by the architect, W. Pope Barney of Philadelphia, for a fieldstone building to harmonize with the neighborhood residences. On July 1, 1936, the cornerstone was laid, and on Sunday morning, January 7, 1937, the first Sunday service and Sunday School were held in the new structure. On November 27, 1938, First Church of Christ, Scientist, Jenkintown, was dedicated. In August of 1933, a Reading Room was opened to the public in

the Liberty Building, Jenkintown, and was moved in 1937 to the present location at 747 Yorkway Place, Jenkintown.

In the early 1970s several alterations were made to make use of the lower level for offices, board and committee rooms. The Sunday School was also remodeled to allow for more class space. These alterations were accomplished with the help of Robert O. Race, a Media architect, and E. Allen Reeves, Inc. of Abington, builders.

The Sunday morning services are conducted to two Readers, elected by and from the membership to serve for three years. Following the singing of hymns and prayer, the Readers read the Lesson-Sermon which consists of excerpts from the Bible and from *Science and Health With Key to the Scriptures* by Mary Baker Eddy.

Mrs. Eddy, the Discoverer and Founder of Christian Science, experienced the sudden healing of an injury in 1866 while reading the New Testament. From that point on, she devoted her life to exploring the relationship between faith and Christian healing as taught by Christ Jesus. Her teachings became the basis for a new denomination. By mid-1870, she had taught her first public class and had copyrighted a manuscript outlining her ideas. In 1875 she published *Science And Health*, which she repeatedly revised over the next 35 years.

In 1879 Mrs. Eddy and a group of fifteen followers founded the Church of Christ, Scientist, with the aim of reinstating "primitive Christianity and its lost element of healing." Within the next decade, the Christian Science movement had grown to national proportions, its stable, long-term growth largely affected through the healing work carried on by students whom Mrs. Eddy instructed. In 1892 the church was reorganized into its present form as The Mother

*Edited by Nancy MacMeekin

Church, The First Church of Christ, Scientist, in Boston, and its branches around the world.

Mrs. Eddy, born in 1821, began her life as a sickly child surrounded by an intellectual and academic family. Because of illness she gained formal education only through a brother who tutored her in all subjects, including the classics. From her intense spiritual experiences and from her perceptions, a new understanding of Christianity developed into a movement that has continued ever since. The insights and knowledge that Mrs. Eddy presented in her written works are studied in depth today by those who seek to understand her vision.

Citations from Mrs. Eddy's *Science And Health* to be read each week are outlined in advance and are studied during the week preceding the Sunday service. The twenty-eight rotating subjects of the lesson-sermons are specified by Mrs. Eddy and include such subjects as "God," "Christ Jesus," "Man," "Love," "Sacrament," "Spirit," "Matter," "Reality," and "Is the Universe, Including Man, Evolved by Atomic Force?"

Wednesday evening meetings include testimonies of healing through Christian Science. At these meetings, the First Reader selects brief readings from the Bible and Science And Health, often relevant to current community or world challenges as well as to personal challenges. Following hymns and prayer, members of the congregation rise spontaneously to give accounts of their own experiences of physical healing and of other problems resolved through prayer. Christian Scientists view this as time to voice their appreciation for God's blessings and care. Annual Thanksgiving Day services are conducted along similar lines.

Christian Science branch churches, which are self-governing, follow Mrs. Eddy's conviction that the church organization itself is most useful when it remains secondary and of service to Christian regeneration and healing. The simple form of Christian Science branch churches, the absence of hierarchy, and the equal status of men and women reflects this conviction.

In the Christian Science Reading Room on Yorkway Place near the center of Jenkintown, one can find the writings of Mary Baker Eddy as well as the three periodicals published by the Mother Church. The Christian Science Sentinel is a weekly periodical, while The Christian Science Journal is published monthly. Many lay people are familiar with The Christian Science Monitor, which is published Monday through Friday. The Monitor, an international daily newspaper, presents in-depth articles covering world news as well as financial analysis, current trends in fashion, book reviews, and editorials. Only one article on the last page is designated as a religious article reflecting the teachings of Christian Science.

Study and prayer continue through a lifetime of involvement with Christian Science. Sunday School begins the process of understanding and includes pupils up to the age of twenty years. The first lessons of the children include the Ten Commandments, the Lord's Prayer and the Sermon on the Mount. Guidance is given to help pupils live and practice Scriptural teachings in their own lives and to learn to heal themselves and help others. These young people join their elders in answering Christ Jesus' call "Follow me."

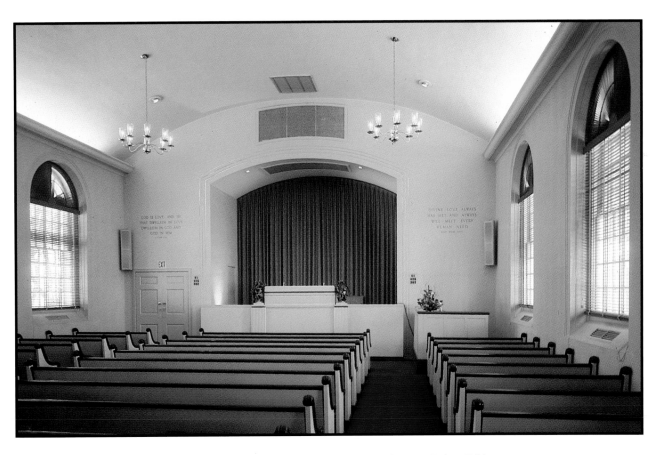

This simple room proclaims the message of Mary Baker Eddy:
"Divine love always has met and always will meet every human need."

First Church of Christ, Scientist

TOUR

The colonial building which houses the First Church of Christ, Scientist, has stood in its present location since 1937. The congregation which studies and faithfully follows the spiritual discovers of Mary Baker Eddy has been at home in the gracious, light-filled building for over half a century.

Fieldstone, common to many buildings in this area, forms the external walls of the Christian Scientist Church. The colonial elements are easily identified. White doric columns flank the main entrance which is capped by a scrolled pediment. Traditional white shutters extend the length of the doorway and are used to frame the windows of the church. With the exception of the wing to the right, where Sunday school is held, the building is appropriately symmetrical in design.

While this congregation has chosen the colonial style in which to frame its church, it is interesting to note that Christian Scientist churches are not required to take any particular architectural style. World wide, the churches have many forms, and some that are built today are modern in style. The religion does not dictate the physical proportions of the church.

On entering the red-carpeted foyer of the church, notice is directed to the stairways on the left and right leading to a balcony that extends the seating capacity for each service. To the right, a passageway leads to the Sunday School wing and leads also downstairs to offices, a board room, and other meeting rooms.

Two doorways allow access to the Auditorium where services take place. Two aisles separate the seating area of the Auditorium. This large room is a model of classic simplicity. From a gently vaulted ceiling hang brass chandeliers that might be found in any Federal-period building. Large Palladian windows punctuate the simple white walls, allowing bursts of sunlight to enter the room. Each window is handled in the same fashion, with the predominant soft Colonial green coloring the blinds and the fan-shaped treatments that fill the circular space at the tops. This fan shape is repeated in the clerestory window that hangs high in the balcony wall. The wooden trim of the pews, dark walnut in the shape of the scroll, repeats the decorative theme of the pediment at the front entrance.

The focal points of the room are not the traditional objects in a typical church. There is no baptismal font or altar. At the front of the room is the platform from which the Sunday morning and Wednesday evening services are conducted. Two Readers, elected by the congregation, stand here to conduct services.

The platform is gently highlighted by three gold bands that are recessed into the wall around the area. On either side of the Reader's Desk are two wooden urns, filled with flowers or plants, that rest on fluted half-columns. To the right of the platform is the new church organ, added in 1987.

On the walls to either side of the platform are important quotations that link Christian Science to its two primary sources. On the left, the words: "*God is Love; And He that Dwelleth in Love Dwelleth in God and God in Him,*" was taken from the New Testament, I John 4:16. To the right Mrs. Eddy's words: "*Divine Love Always Has Met and Always Will Meet Every Human Need,*" reminds the congregation of an important premise of Christian Science.

There are small rooms upstairs, directly above the platform where the First and Second Reader prepare themselves spiritually for the service that follows. In one small room and in the Christian Science Reading Room there hangs a portrait of Mrs. Eddy, respected as a teacher, leader and founder of the movement. Her portrait will not be found in the public areas of the church which are devoted to the worship of God.

Front of Auditorium with quotation by Mary Baker Eddy.

In the wing to the right of the Auditorium, Sunday School classes are held during the time services are held. In one large room, filled with round tables and colonial-style chairs, both the Bible and *Science and Health With Key to the Scriptures* are studied. Like the Auditorium there is a quotation from the New Testament on the left and Mrs. Eddy's words repeated on the right, etched into the wall. This room provides a simple, light-filled atmosphere for learning to take place.

As part of the by-laws of The Mother Church, The First Church of Christ, Scientist in Boston, Massachusetts, each branch church must establish a Reading Room which provides a place to welcome the public. The Jenkintown Reading Room offers an unhurried atmosphere in which to study the elements of Christian Science. The Reading Room is seen as a ministry, an open door, to the public. Information and, above all, an understanding of Divine Love is expressed to all who enter. The Reading Room provides access to the writings of Mrs. Eddy and to the Christian Science periodicals published regularly by The Mother Church in Boston, Massachusetts.

Upper room with portrait of Mrs. Eddy.

In the simple Auditorium of the First Church of Christ, Scientist, and in the Reading Room, this congregation joins with others throughout the world who study and live the Christian Science life.

Publications displayed outside Reading Room.

Abington Friends Meeting

Abington Friends Meeting

Meetinghouse Road and Greenwood Avenue, Jenkintown

HISTORY*

In 1983, Abington Friends Meeting, the oldest congregation in the area treated in this book, celebrated its 300th anniversary. The first religious services of the Religious Society of Friends in this vicinity were held December 3, 1683, in the house of Richard Wall, on York Road at Church Road. The present grounds of 120 acres were acquired, in 1697, through the gift of John Barnes, a Quaker landowner with extensive holdings. The land grant was accompanied by a financial grant of fifty pounds to build a meetinghouse and 150 pounds to start a school.

Monthly Meetings for Business were being held at Abington by 1702. The building, completed with the assistance of other Meetings in the area, was probably being used by 1699 or 1700. Religious and business meetings have been held at this location ever since. The original Meetinghouse was enlarged as membership increased. The eastern half of the present building was erected in 1786, probably using part of the walls of the original Meetinghouse. The present western half dates from 1798. An addition known as the John Barnes Building was completed in 1929; the East Wing, in 1966. Abington Friends School, now an extensive multi-building complex, was originally housed in the Meetinghouse. Not until 1784 did it make the first of its moves, to what is now the caretaker's house.

The founder of the Religious Society of Friends was George Fox, an Englishman who was dissatisfied with the Established Church of the mid-seventeenth century. As a result of his spiritual struggles, he concluded that each person is capable of reaching God directly, without clergy as an intermediary. If there are no clergy, there is no need for a pulpit. If all

of life is sacramental, outward observance of sacraments is not necessary, and there is no need for altars, baptismal fonts, and other features of many places of worship. William Penn, whose Pennsylvania colony was a "Holy Experiment," was a follower of George Fox. Penn summed up the Friends' faith in these words: "The less form in religion the better, since God is a Spirit."

Abington Friends, whose Meeting goes back to more than a century before the adoption of the Constitution, worship, as did Friends of those early days, in a large, unadorned room. They meet on the basis of expectant waiting in silence. Out of the silence spoken messages sometimes come. There is no programmed service, no recitation of prayers, no sermon, no music. Those who share a spoken message may do so in the form of a prayer, a reading from the Bible, or, occasionally, a song. Before the Meeting for Worship itself, there are classes for children and adults. Hymn singing is a regular part of these sessions. The Meeting for Worship ends when Friends on the facing bench in the front of the room shake hands and others then follow suit.

The Meeting for Worship, unusual as it may seem to one who is unfamiliar with it, is not so distinctive as are Friends' Meetings for Business, which are held each month. To quote William Penn again: "True Godliness does not drive men out of the world but rather enables them to live in it and excites their endeavors to mend it." The "endeavors to mend it" are the putting of beliefs into action, and the Meeting for Business is the starting point. Here an individual Friend may present a concern in the hope of receiving the support of the Meeting as a whole to proceed with a plan of action. A committee representative's report on the work of the committee may include a recommendation for action by the Meeting. Whenever an

We are grateful to Marjorie M. Anderson for preparing the history.

action is to be taken, all Friends are encouraged to express their views. No votes are taken. The presiding clerk has the responsibility of determining what the "sense of the meeting" is and how the Meeting should proceed. No action will be taken if the Meeting is not in unity.

Friends' belief that there is "that of God" in everyone has led many of them to oppose slavery, war, and capital punishment. It has led them to work for better prison conditions and improved treatment of those in mental hospitals. Abington Meeting has had its share of involvement in many of these efforts. As early as the 1730's it had a member, Benjamin Lay, who was a vigorous and sometimes dramatic protestor against slavery. Over the years, its members have shown their concern for social justice in many ways. They have been involved with their local community and with the world community. Through membership on committees of the Philadelphia Yearly Meeting, they join forces with others to work for the goals that they believe are important. Frequent committee meetings are the common experience of many Friends. In the absence of a hierarchy, much responsibility rests on each individual Friend, and committees are the vehicles for carrying out these responsibilities.

Abington Friends Meeting has diversity within its unity, as do most Friends Meetings, since there is no formal creed to which all must subscribe. A letter from the Meeting of Elders at Balby, written in 1656, is as applicable today as it was more than three hundred years ago:

> Dearly beloved Friends, these things we do not lay upon you as a rule or form to walk by, but that all, with the measure of light which is pure and holy, may be guided; and so in the light walking and abiding, these may be fulfilled in the Spirit, not in the letter, for the letter killeth, but the Spirit giveth life.

*Here Friends have gathered for almost three
hundred years, "centering down" to reach their spiritual depths.*

Abington Friends Meeting

TOUR

The Meetinghouse of the Abington Friends is a two-story stone building set horizontally along a piece of land deeded to them in 1697. There are no external markings that proclaim this building to be a church, no spire, no bell tower, no stretching transept to announce its Christian roots. It has a simple exterior, unadorned except for the porch extension, added in 1863, that extends across its front. To the left are later additions that provide space for classes and for the monthly Meeting for Business.

The building is a Meetinghouse typical of others in the area, its basic structure reflecting the beliefs of the group. The Quaker movement began in 1652 when George Fox envisioned a sharply different way to worship God. Friends, like many others, came to the New World to seek religious freedom. However, even in this new country, Quakers were persecuted for their differences. Pennsylvania became a haven for the group who were holding Meetings for Worship in the Cheltenham area as early as 1682. It was only fifty years after George Fox's radical vision that the religious group, backed by a gift of land and money, built the first Meetinghouse in Jenkintown.

Dedicated to the word of Christ, Quakers stripped away the rituals and ceremonies of the established church, seeking a more direct communication with God. Ministers were believed to be unnecessary as each person housed the divine within him. Thus Meetings were held on the basis of silent expectation, allowing the individual to reach inward, to open himself to God and to respond spontaneously to "that of God" within. Those practices of worship continue in this Meetinghouse today.

The Meeting for Worship takes place within the one large room. The Meetinghouse itself is not considered to be a sacred place as the whole world is believed to be sacred and blessed. There is no creed in

Original eighteenth-century doors.

this church, only a series of tenets that form the basis of the religion. Testimonies of Community, Peace and Equality have stimulated Quakers to work against slavery and war. Recently this Meeting's projects have included supporting an immigrant Cambodian family and raising money to rebuild a destroyed medical clinic in Sebokeng, South Africa. The testimony of Simplicity is what defines the physical Meetinghouse as well as the worship service.

Enter the Meetinghouse to view a physical extension of one major belief. Even at first glance, the complete simplicity of the large room used by the

Religious Society of Friends for worship will be apparent. Flights of stairs jut to the right and left of the entrance to lead to the galleries overhead, to the balconies that extend from three of the four walls. There are the benches below that, unlike other places of worship, are turned so people can face each other. In fact, in more modern Meetinghouses, the benches are often placed in a semicircle so there is no head, no person or group that is more important than another. Here, however, two rows of facing benches, those directly opposite the entrance, are placed as in the old tradition, elevated somewhat to allow everyone to see whoever is speaking. Towards the rear wall, also, the benches have been elevated for the same reason.

There is no focal point, no visual area for concentration, in the Meetinghouse as there are in other churches. The altar, pulpit, lectern, and baptismal font have not been included. Between the facing benches are flowers placed there for each Sunday's Meeting. Behind the flowers are two chairs that are moved forward during weddings, to be occupied by the couple to be married. Weddings as well as funerals are occasions that begin with a period of worship.

The first Meetinghouse existed to the right of the entrance. That section, used from 1699 to 1797 was torn down because of a need for more space. The original stone was used to build the current room. In 1798 the Meetinghouse was again enlarged with the west addition. Notice the wall that separates the gallery in half. In the past there was a dividing door that came down from the ceiling on ropes and pulleys to make two rooms out of the one large one. Women's Meetings for Worship were held on one side, and men's on the other. This practice was abolished in the late 1800s.

Other evidence of past practices can be found on the beams that support the rear gallery. Notice the darkened wood of these beams. Four huge pot-bellied stoves once stood at the foot of each, with their elongated stove pipes reaching to the ceiling above. Four round holes remain where the pipes exited for exhaust.

Behind the facing benches, where the elders of the church sat in times past, are two doors that are opened during the warmer months. It is on these doors and on the ones used for entry into the Meetinghouse that you can sense the age of the building. The original

The wedding chairs.

hardware is in place and the old nails used to put the doors together remain.

Like the building, the stories of Abington Friends stretch back for centuries. Minutes from the original meetings are housed at the Friends Historical Library at Swarthmore. It is known that the first teacher at the new Quaker school was George Boone, uncle of Daniel Boone. It is remembered that the Friends so desperately needed to raise funds in the early 1800s that they decided to sell the groves of oak trees that surrounded the Meetinghouse to raise money. The Fisher family, still in this area, bought the timber, but never cut down a tree. Some of the massive oaks not felled by hurricanes or disease remain today.

Meetings for Business, similar in form to the old town meetings in early settlements, are held each month. Each member of the Meeting can participate in these meetings. Friends here then meet with Friends during the Quarterly Meeting that draw groups from several other Meetings that comprise the Quarter. Finally there are the yearly meetings of the larger regional organizations. Philadelphia Yearly Meeting includes approximately 100 Monthly Meetings. Joint projects that affect the worldwide Quaker organiza-tions are discussed and decisions are made regarding action to be taken.

It is difficult to forget history as you sit in the Meet-inghouse, difficult not to realize how revolutionary George Fox's vision had been in the seventeenth century. It is difficult to imagine that Friends were imprisoned and even tortured in England and even here in the New World that had promised freedom. But Philadelphia had become a sanctuary, where William Penn was able to establish his community without conflict, and where The Religious Society of Friends flourished.

In this simple room and in others similar to it, with its wooden wainscotting and wooden benches, with the large windows that allow sunlight to flood in, and with angles of steps and galleries added to hold more of the congregation, Friends have gathered for more than three hundred years. They have entered in silence, "centering down," to reach into their own spiritual depths. They have listened to the words of God flowing through another Friend, and they have offered, from time to time, their own understanding of life as their faith has shaped it.

John Greenleaf Whittier, nineteenth century

"For deeper rest to this still room."

Quaker poet, captured the quiet power of the Meeting for Worship when he wrote:

> *And so I find it well to come*
> *For deeper rest to this still room,*
> *For here the habit of the soul*
> *Feels less the outer world's control;*
> *The strength of mutual purpose pleads*
> *More earnestly our common needs;*
> *And from the silence multiplied*

> *By these still forms on either side,*
> *The world that time and sense have known*
> *Falls off and leaves us God alone.*
> — *The Clear Vision*

Listen to the silence. Hear the old clock ticking in unity with time and understanding. Feel the presence of faith here as did the Friends of the past and as do the Friends of today.

Immaculate Conception Church

Immaculate Conception Church

Summit Avenue and Leedom Street, Jenkintown

HISTORY

A few Catholics had settled in Eastern Pennsylvania farming districts by the late eighteenth century. By the mid-nineteenth century, when seventy Catholic families lived in and around Jenkintown, Bishop John Neumann (now Saint John Neumann) of the Philadelphia Archdiocese authorized the purchase of a lot within the Borough on August 8, 1857 on which a church could be built. This L-shaped ground, bounded by West Avenue, Cedar and Leedom Streets, and Greenwood Avenue still remains the heart of Immaculate Conception Parish.

It would be some time, however, before a Catholic church would become a reality. Until 1864, priests from Chestnut Hill came to Jenkintown once a month to offer Mass in Lyceum Hall which served all denominations as a place of worship from the 1850s until churches could be built. Then for two years St. Mary's Church, the early name for the new parish, was attached as a mission to St. Joachim's Church in the Frankford section of Philadelphia. Priests from there came to the Lyceum to say Mass for parishioners each Sunday.

The year 1866 marks the founding date of Immaculate Conception Parish, for early in that year a temporary frame church was built on the Greenwood side of the property, and its first pastor, Reverend Thomas P. Toner, arrived in February to begin the building of a real parish. Father Toner, a native of Ireland and only twenty-six years old, performed the first baptism in the parish on February 11 and the first marriage on February 24, 1866.

With much labor supplied by parishioners, a stone church facing West Avenue was constructed and its cornerstone laid on July 15, 1866. Father Toner offered the first Mass there on March 17, 1867 for worshipers sitting on rough boards because there were no pews or kneeling benches.

From Father Toner's time up to the present, 124 years in all, Immaculate Conception has had only seven pastors. Each one not only constructed buildings but also endeared himself to the families involved in building a true parish spirit.

One of the outstanding pastors was Reverend Joseph A. Strahan, who served from 1892 to 1915. He built the first parish school, a one-story structure on Cedar Street behind the church. It opened in 1893 with twenty-six students taught by two lay teachers and himself.

In 1898, five Sisters of St. Joseph arrived to take charge of the school, beginning a long term of service to the parish. Father Strahan built a new rectory and remodeled the old one on Cedar Street to accommodate the Sisters. By 1905, the school contained ninety-eight boys and eighty-four girls and had gained commendation from the Board of Public Education for its high standards of teaching. A needed second story was soon added.

The parish by then had grown in numbers. Three Masses were offered each Sunday for congregants arriving from as far away as Glenside, Willow Grove, Fox Chase, Elkins Park and Oak Lane.

Early in the morning of February 1, 1928, fire destroyed the church. At 3:45 a.m. the blaze was discovered by Mrs. Patric Wade from across the street and milkman John Waddington, who aroused the rectory and convent after turning in an alarm. Twenty-one fire companies, from Philadelphia, Ogontz, McKinley, Abington, Roslyn, Weldon, Glenside, Edge Hill, and LaMott fought the blaze and confined it to the church. Nearby residents opened their homes and served food and hot coffee to the firefighters.

The shock and exposure in the frigid night while personally overseeing the safety of personnel and buildings, and then the extended efforts in rebuilding, left the pastor, Reverend John E. Cavanaugh, in poor health. He died on June 26, 1929.

His successor, Right Reverend Monsignor Thomas F. McNally, L.L.D., arrived to face the numerous problems involved in the final restoration of the church and needed improvements that had been delayed because of Father Cavanaugh's illness. The new church was completed and ready for use within two months of Monsignor's arrival and was dedicated on September 22. Monsignor McNally immediately concluded negotiations for the purchase of a lot adjoining the church property on the east and two old buildings which he had torn down for a larger school yard.

He bought a bus to transport the children living in the outskirts of the parish and signed on sexton John J. Jennings as bus driver, among other duties. John Jennings recently retired after fifty-eight years of service. Three more Sisters of St. Joseph joined the staff. In the 1960s, as enrollment increased to 500, Monsignor McNally built a modern three-story school next to the rectory in the space that had been the playground. The old school was then torn down and the space behind the church became a parking lot.

In his thirty-eight years as pastor of Immaculate Conception Church, Monsignor McNally did much to encourage the spiritual and intellectual life of parishioners and was respected and admired by Catholics and non-Catholics in the community. He died Sunday, September 10, 1967.

Within days a successor was appointed, the Reverend Monsignor William H. Flatley. Msgr. Flatley carried on the tradition of selfless service to God, Church and community, woven through the history of Immaculate Conception Church in Jenkintown. Early in his pastorate, he brought together two elements of parish life important to the progress and upkeep of the church. He established the Women's Guild to be responsible for social functions and the Home and School Association, concerned with interaction between parents and faculty.

Monsignor Flatley kept all the church properties in excellent condition. He added greater parking and playground space by acquiring the old Borough Hall

property to the east of the school in 1981. 1988 was the last year that the school enjoyed the presence of nuns. The Sisters of St. Joseph, who had served continually since 1898, withdrew because of the scarcity of vocations.

Monsignor Flatley's greatest gift to his parish was his spirituality in his love of God. Wherever solace is needed, he was there. He celebrated the Golden Jubliee of his Ordination on May 31, 1987 with a Mass and dinner with 600 parishioners and friends gathered to help him celebrate most joyfully.

The following year Monsignor Flately was named Pastor Emeritus and Rev. John J. Conahan was appointed his successor. Father Conahan arrived in Jenkintown just as Most Rev. Anthony J. Bevilacqua was installed as Archbishop of Philadelphia. The new ordinary divided the Archdiocese into vicariates and introduced a new organizational structure for its administration.

In keeping with the spirit of re-structure at the diocesan level, Father Conahan formed a committee of parishioners to study the parish community preliminary to the formation of a Pastoral Council. He completed a renovation of the Church started by Monsignor Flately giving particular attention to unifying the altars to make the sanctuary more liturgically correct. In the process, the Church was recarpeted and some of the exquisite Mercer tiles which cover the floor of the sanctuary and aisles were exposed and lacquered.

Father Conahan had several Eucharistic Ministers commissioned to bring Communion to the housebound after Sunday Mass and ramped the side entrance to the Church to make it accessible to the handicapped.

In 1991 Father Conahan will lead the Immaculate Conception Parish in a joyful celebration of 125 years of service. Many assistant priests, nuns, and countless parishioners and friends have been part of the work of Immaculate Conception Parish. From its beginning in 1866 as St. Mary's, through its renaming in 1881, and to the present, Immaculate Conception Parish has been a vital part of Jenkintown community life.

The eye is directed upwards in this Romanesque church, towards the
large wooden crucifix suspended above the intersection of the nave and the transept.

Immaculate Conception Church

TOUR

It is a dramatic story: the fire destroying the original church that had been in existence since 1886, the fire engines rushing to the scene in the cold of that February morning early in 1928, the impact of the destroyed church upon the Roman Catholic parish of Jenkintown. But the religious tradition of Immaculate Conception continues in the church that was built in 1929 on the ashes of the first.

From the outside the church does not reveal the impact of design that is immediately apparent on entering the nave. Here are all the details of the Romanesque style, a movement in architecture that predated the Gothic period of the Middle Ages and has been repeated in church architecture since then. This church is filled with rounded rather than pointed forms.

Typically, Romanesque churches feature geometric regularity, and the pattern holds true here. The repeated circular rhythms can be seen in the barrel-shaped roof as well as in the arches that mark the length of the nave. The roof, divided into sections of ribs of geometrically painted wood, is covered primarily by rectangles of pressed wood that have been structured into a herringbone pattern. The eye is led high into the building and towards the large wooden crucifix that hangs suspended above the intersection of the nave and the transept.

The nave is flanked by two aisles of columns, connected by rounded archways that lead towards the altar. There is room for the congregation to pass here, moving between the walls of the building and the pews in a pattern reminiscent of the ancient church ambulatory circuit. The columns are beautiful, almost free-standing sculpture in themselves, as they rise to intricate Corinthian capitals. These columns are made of marble but of alternating colors, green and brown, adding the richness of the stone to the

Angel prays above the church columns.

total effect. Above each column, angels soar in space. Recently restored, the brilliance of the gold wash behind the angels is very apparent. These angels pray in the great space of the vault, with their wings stretched upward, circling behind them.

Behind the columns, along the walls of the nave, are two other decorative elements. The most familiar is the use of stained glass. In this church, the windows tell the story of Jesus in a circular fashion. The Annunciation is treated in a large window in the south transept. The story continues in the windows that move clockwise around the church, beginning along the south wall and finally ending in the large north transept window. The final window, that hangs directly opposite the Annunciation, shows the coming of the Holy Spirit. Mary is in the middle of the window with the Apostles around her. Above her head is the Holy Spirit appearing in the traditional form of the dove.

What is most interesting about these windows is the double story they tell. The upper, more dominant sections portray the story of Jesus, but the lower scenes depict stories from the Old Testament, as if to remind the viewer of the roots of Christianity.

In between the windows molded reliefs are set into the walls. Because of the brilliant blue background, the intricate plaster scenes jump out in three-dimensional drama. These scenes portray the Fourteen Stations of the Cross, seven along the north wall and seven along the south. They can be read in reverse order from the windows, starting with the first scene at the top of the north wall, just before the transept, with Pilate washing his hands to indicate that he was innocent of Jesus' death. The Passion moves counter clockwise around the church and ends on the south wall, directly opposite, where Jesus is taken down from the cross for burial.

Other holy personages are remembered in the church. On either side of the west end doors are painted tiles added in 1977 to commemorate two recently canonized saints; St. Elizabeth Seton, a convert who founded schools for poor children, and Philadelphia's Bishop St. John Newmann, who worked among the poor immigrants, take their places of honor.

Pass below the suspended crucifix. Glance to left and to the right, to notice the complete geometric regularity of this part of the church. What appears in one transept is repeated, honoring different religious figures, in the other. Turn towards the north transept to the marble baptismal font to the left. Notice that the different colored marble columns on the font echo the shape and colors of the columns of the communion rail that passes the length of the transept. Above the font is the final window of the Jesus story, and to the right is the altar of the Sacred Heart. In this area of the church there is also a very special floor of tile laid by the Mercer Tile Company of Doylestown

Jesus, with the symbol of the Sacred Heart, stands above the marble altar.

with intricate patterns and symbols.

This altar, like the others in the church, is intricately fashioned of marble and mosaic tiles. The tiles, set in the base, surround a contrasting colored marble on which the symbol of the Sacred Heart is formed by pieces of painted stone. The greens, blues, and golds of the tiles provide a backdrop for the red tiles, representing the heart itself which is on fire, flames rising from within. Jesus stands above the altar with His hands open to the congregation. On His chest the heart symbol is repeated as the statue depicts the love Jesus holds for humanity. Next to Jesus stand massive silver-plated, iron candle sticks, among the few things to escape the 1928 fire.

Stand now before the Altar of Sacrifice. You will notice two marble statues flanking the sanctuary. To the left is St. Joseph and to the right, St. Anthony. Look to the south transept to see the first of the Jesus windows, the Annunciation, showing Mary accept-

The Sanctuary, altar rail and Mercer tiles.

ing the word of God. Her answer, *"Behold, I am the handmaid of the Lord,"* is captured in the glass. Next to this window is another altar, similar to the Sacred Heart, on which stands a statue of the Blessed Virgin. But in front of you is the most intricate altar in the church.

The sanctuary has two altars that originally had been one. On the front of the smaller Altar of Sacrifice, spelled in mosaics, are the Greek symbols for Alpha and Omega, representing the belief that Jesus is the beginning and the end. In the middle is another Christian symbol, the lamb. Behind the other altar the reredos rises into its own Romanesque architecture with a large gilded dome that stands on its own columns. On either side, two intricately carved wooden angels that have been gold-leafed, kneel with wings uplifted behind them.

On the wall behind the altar is one final tribute to the Virgin Mary, the patroness of this church. The panel is outlined by a border of brilliant red and gold design. She stands above the congregation, with the blue sky behind her and angels to her side. With raised hands, she blesses the congregation before her. If you look closely, you will see a part of the painting that is almost obscured by the massive altar. Below Mary is the family tree of Jesse, depicting, as does the bottom half of the windows, Jesus' roots in the Old Testament.

The Church of Immaculate Conception is rich in its architectural details and rich in its acts of charity. Within its walls are a continuing reaffirmation of faith after the devastating fire. In vivid details the story of Jesus is told through scenes set in glass and plaster. Christ is suspended above in a powerfully felt, massive cross. And the Blessed Virgin rises behind the altar to watch over all.

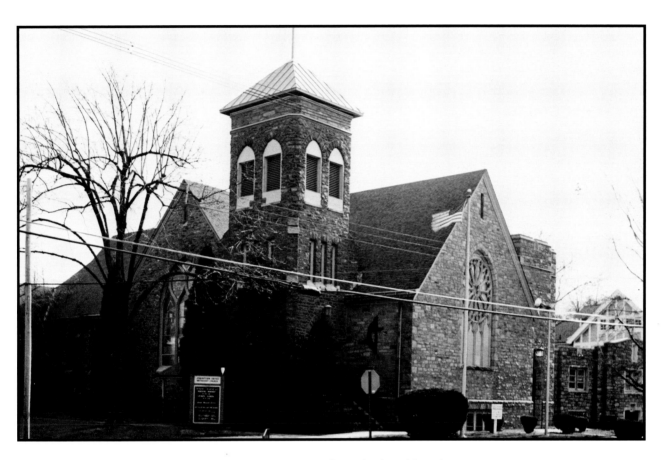

Jenkintown United Methodist Church

HISTORY*

Methodism was introduced into Philadelphia in the year 1769 by the Rev. Dr. Joseph Pilmore, having then arrived on a preaching mission from John Wesley. John Wesley had not organized a separate religious group but had mainly differed with the established Anglican Church on certain points. Methodism of that day collected people of any faith and required no other rule of association than a desire to worship God.

The Methodists of that day were not distinguished by such violent emotions and bodily exercises in their assemblies as occurred in meetings at a later period. General practices of the early church included an emphasis on congregational singing. An early description gave this description: "Methodists poured forth a stream of vehement song in exultant triumph, often standing about the altar, mixed together like joyous birds on a tree top."

Methodist meetings were held as early as 1834 and 1839 in a hall in Jenkintown. The first recorded minutes list January 28, 1842 as the date when the Lyceum was used for long services and revivals. Methodist ministers traveled by horse or coach from Milestown (now Oak Lane) or Germantown to conduct these services.

In 1866 Jenkintown was a small community, and three of the resident families were members of Milestown Methodist Episcopal church. They and others saw the need for a local Methodist Church. During the summer of 1867 the public school house on West Street in Jenkintown was offered for sale. The building was purchased, remodeled and dedicated for the worship of God on September 14, 1867.

In these early and formative years Jenkintown shared preachers with other churches in the district,

with varying combinations on the circuits. On some Sundays there would be lay speakers when the preacher could not get to the appointed service.

1879-1880 brought to a climax a building problem and a financial crisis that had been plaguing the Church. The condition of the small and inconvenient building had become such that it was necessary to use an umbrella for protection in church on rainy days. How to liquidate the debt and build a new church seemed an unanswerable question to the disheartened believers. A request was granted by the Annual Conference to relieve the church from paying a pastor's salary for one year. Plans were then made, and the Church was enlarged and repaired. The dedication was held on December 28, 1879.

This period inaugurated a time of growth in membership. The Rev. George H. Lorah served Jenkintown during the years 1885-1887. By 1895 the trustees realized that the church was well-established, and a corporate charter was granted.

At the corporation meeting of the church on March 30, 1897, the trustees were authorized to sell the church property and build elsewhere. The church was purchased by Jenkintown to serve as the Borough Hall, and the new church was to be located at Summit Avenue and Walnut Streets. Dedication services were held from October 26 to November 2, 1902. An additional lot on Walnut Street was acquired for the new parsonage.

Additions and improvements to the new church continued well into the twentieth century. In the early 1920s electric lighting was added, a new bell was placed in the tower, and a social hall and kitchen were added. In 1952 an enlargement of the church took place that changed the interior to the one that exists today. During the time the remodeling was in progress, Sunday services were conducted in the chapel of

---

*Edited by W. Berkeley MacKenney, Jr.

Beaver College, which was then located in Jenkintown across from the Jenkintown railroad station. The cornerstone for the new additions was laid on December 6, 1953. On March 7, 1954 the opening service was held in the new sanctuary.

A voice amplification system was added in 1957. With the appointment of a resident Associate Pastor, the house at 143 Walnut Street was purchased in August 1958. Again the increase in church membership and expansion of services indicated a need for more space, and in 1961 Fellowship House was razed in order to erect an Education Building. The removal of Fellowship House necessitated the relocation of the church office and pastor's study, which were then installed in the main church edifice. In December of 1964 a carillon was installed as a memorial.

During 1969 a new parsonage for the Senior Pastor was purchased at 505 Elm Avenue. With the transfer of the Associate Pastor and his family to 145 Walnut Street, the land was cleared for an enlarged parking lot.

In 1968 the church came to be known as Jenkintown United Methodist Church because of a merger of the former Methodist Church and the former Evangelical United Brethren Church. The United Methodist Church is the second largest Protestant denomination in the United States with 9,200,000 members in seventy-three annual conferences and more than 35,000 local churches. Since 1968 the church's activities have been a lively and vital witness in the community. While growth is slow at this time, the church remains strong.

Children from the community, including many of different ethnic and religious backgrounds, attend preschool. The Food Cupboard, along with the Opportunities Board of Montgomery County, collects nonperishables to distribute to needy families.

For the governing philosophy is to offer the church as a community center, to make the church a rallying place for the good of the community as a whole.

The church also hosts college choirs and occasional concerts during the worship service. At these times an orchestra is added and the choir performs major works as an act of worship. Twice a month the Senior Friends meet for luncheon at the church. This group draws seniors from all religions and from the broad base of southeastern Montgomery County and offers fellowship to 50-60 people. In addition, the church is open to electoral candidates who often address interested groups here. And the church supports thirty-eight Methodist mission projects around the world.

The Jenkintown United Methodist Church has served the community well, and has been served well by several distinguished ministers. The Rev. Dr. Paul W. Poley saw the largest growth in the congregation, from 350 when he came in 1943 to well over 750 when he left in 1953. Dr. Poley became a District Superintendent upon leaving. The Rev. Charles Scott Kerr increased the membership to over 900 and began a pastorate which included several associate ministers. He went on to serve one of the largest congregations in our conference, First United Methodist of Lancaster. The Rev. Dr. Stacy Meyers, Jr. was much loved by congregation and community alike, leaving the church to assume the responsibilities of the District Superintendency. The Rev. Robert L. Jones, The Rev. Gerald F. Crowell, and The Rev. Robert A. Mongold provided fine leadership in recent years. On July 1, 1988, Dr. Daniel Ellis-Killian assumed the responsibility of Senior Minister of this congregation which has such a rich and vital heritage in our community.

*A great Gothic arch frames the reredos and the
beautiful rose window, each of whose twelve petals reminds one of the Trinity.*

Jenkintown United Methodist Church

TOUR

Jenkintown Methodist originally was a neighborhood church, a place of worship easily accessible by foot. In 1867 only a few had to take horse and buggy to reach the church when it occupied the old school house next to Immaculate Conception. The desire to keep Jenkintown Methodist close to the growing Jenkintown community prompted the move to Summit Avenue and Walnut Street in 1902 when more space was needed. The "English" country church still stands at this location but now draws worshippers from many different areas of the larger community.

Along the exterior walls of the church the interested visitor can find four corner stones that mark the various expansions of the building. The 1869 cornerstone from the original church was incorporated into the newer building. In 1902 the church existed without the chancel which was added in 1952. 1961 marked further expansions.

The interior of the church is both Victorian and Gothic in style. Originally the Akron plan of church structure was followed. A common architectural form of Protestant churches in the late nineteenth century, it produced pulpit-centered churches, without

the chancel that is present today.

At this time the church is oriented towards the north, with the chancel facing north instead of the traditional eastern direction. Originally the pulpit stood where the piano now rests. The west transept, then, did not contain the stained glass window as it does now. Rather the archway was open as part of the preaching platform. Now the window depicting Christ laying hands on the little children fills the space. It serves to separate the transept from the small chapel that occupies the space behind. Walk directly in front of the communion rail, marking the width of the church from the east wall towards this west wall. You will feel the downward slope of the floor purposely installed in the original building to allow each worshipper an easy view of the pulpit.

In 1952, the decision was made to follow the cruciform church design predominant in the Oxford Movement. This style was popular from the early 1900s to the 1950s and patterned churches on the ideas of the Gothic scholars in England. To enhance the church at this point, the chancel was built. The pulpit and the lectern were moved to where they are

Four cornerstones recall the enlargements of the church.

Christ laying hands on the little children.

now today; the high altar in the chancel was added with the baptismal font placed to the right; and the communion rail was stretched across the front of the church.

In this church, as in other Methodist churches, the worship service focuses on a movement of the worshipper towards the altar. Communion is taken at the communion rail; prayer and confirmation and vows of membership take place near the altar, as do baptisms. Thus this part of the church has become the primary focal point.

The many stained glass windows here contain recognizable symbols of the Christian faith. Beginning on the west wall, there is the anchor interwoven with the cross, showing Christianity as the anchor of faith. The two tablets of the Ten Commandments are the basis of the old covenant upon which the new covenant was built. The cross and lilies are the symbols of the Resurrection with the scroll identifying Christ's virtues of hope, faith and charity. Then the sheaf of

wheat represents the harvest of those who are the members of the church. The cross and crown show Christ as king while the lamb and the cross refer to Christ as the lamb of God. Chi and Rho as well as Alpha and Omega are Greek letters that refer to Jesus.

The large window in the transept facing east shows an intricate tableau of one element of Christ's early ministry. Here Jesus is in the home of Mary and Martha in Bethany. He has visited Lazarus whose sisters now await Jesus. Mary is at His foot, listening to Him teach. Martha serves Jesus but is angry that her sister is not assisting her. Where Martha is tending to household tasks, Mary is eagerly listening to Jesus' words. Christ points out that Mary is the one who has found something of more value.

The window functions almost as a painting showing the details of everyday life. In the architecture of the house the texture of wood, the veining of marble, the intricacies of the decorative roof line, the mark-

Jesus at the home of Mary and Martha.

ings of the stone walls, the green of the tiled floor, are all precisely drawn. It is a multi-leveled room, with Jesus and Mary in the foreground and Martha on the platform towards the rear of the room. Before her the luxuriant tablecloth is covered with pitchers of drink and with bowls of food.

Behind the figures, three arches open widely to show the Palestinian landscape beautifully drawn and disappearing into the perspective of the ongoing space. Here the landscape reflects the Victorian sensibility, as the land shown here depicts the arid condition of the Holy Land during the 1800s. During the time of Jesus, the landscape was lush and densely filled with greenery.

But the focus of the window is Jesus and Mary. She leans forward, enraptured as if to capture His words. There is an overpowering sense of calm here. Jesus is dressed in the only brilliant color of the window, his scarlet robe easily setting him apart. His face is highlighted as he reaches out, offering his ministry not to multitudes, but to two simple women in the intimacy of their home. It is a moment of intense understanding but also of peace. Above the Gothic spires, the anchor, the cross, and the crown repeat the traditional symbols, and the descending dove at the top calls forth the Holy Spirit.

Within the chancel Gothic elements, in addition to the hammer-headed wooden trusses that transverse the ceiling, are found. Behind the High Altar, the reredos is obviously Gothic. The scrolling on the altar is the grapevine, as faith in Jesus is believed to be like a growing vine. The first three letters of the name of Jesus also appear in Greek. The Gothic elements in this Victorian church build a vaultedness to produce an aura of the holy and sacred.

In the wall above the Altar, framed by a Gothic arch, hangs a massive rose window. The rose window has often been found in churches since medieval times; the biblical reference to the Rose of Sharon is the source for these windows. Repeated geometric forms build the petals of the rose. However, within each petal, three red roses can be seen as a statement of the Trinity. Executed by the Willet studios, the window contains many vibrant colors with greens, reds, and yellows forming the center of the flower. But the color blue is all intense, filling the outer petals with many different shades of this color that can be best appreciated in natural light.

Jenkintown Methodist also makes use of the small chapel formed when the chancel was added. A library and a museum containing such memorabilia as Victorian communion sets and old photographs are also housed in the church building. One historical element of the original church has been incorporated into the chapel. Above the altar hangs a cross that is illuminated by electricity. It first hung over the platform in the original church.

Jenkintown Methodist continues the tradition begun by the early settlers in this small community. But at this time the church reaches out from the nucleus that saw its beginnings. It now speaks to the community, not only in the immediate vicinity, but in Philadelphia as well. There is an intentional yoked relationship with the black church of Emmanuel United Methodist that sponsors pulpit and choir exchanges, interchanged Bible studies and retreats.

And yet the founding philosophy continues to govern. Worship, as was believed then and accepted now, should be a proclamation done boldly. In this way the worshipper can find spiritual uplift and renewal through a sense of commitment. Jenkintown Methodist focuses on this strong belief.

Salem Baptist Church

Salem Baptist Church

610 Summit Avenue, Jenkintown

HISTORY

In 1863 Abraham Lincoln, President of the United States, signed the Emancipation Proclamation, an instrument designed to set at liberty four million black people in this country. Emancipation was confirmed with the adoption of the Thirteenth Amendment and the conclusion of the Civil War in 1865. The movement to heal the wounds and scars of a nation torn asunder by fratricidal brutality had begun.

Just nineteen years after the signing of the Emancipation Proclamation, a small group of black people gathered in the home of Mr. and Mrs. Henry Porter on Division Street, Jenkintown, for a Prayer Service. Some of these people had themselves known or knew people who had felt the sting of the days of slavery. Theirs had been lives filled with pain and suffering, followed by joy and happiness. There was a common desire for a place set aside for worship to Almighty God.

As the Prayer Meetings at the Porters' home continued and attendance increased, the people began to realize the need for a larger place in which to worship. The lay leaders turned to Rev. J.D. Brooks, pastor of the Enon Baptist Church of Germantown, for counsel and direction. Rev. Brooks organized the group into a Church and gave them the name "Salem" which means a place of peace.

For several years itinerant ministers served the congregation. Pastor Brooks continued to conduct worship services, deliver sermons and serve communion. The church continued to grow, a singing school was organized, and the group began to hold services in the Jenkintown Lyceum. Rev. Clayton Coles served as pastor for a short time, and it was under his leadership that the present site on Summit Avenue was purchased.

The Rev. H.G. Lee, a brilliant young minister, was called as the first regular pastor of Salem in 1890. He was only twenty-seven years of age. Salem experienced an unprecedented growth under his leadership, and the first church building was erected. Rev. Lee died ten years later, but many of his living descendants are still part of the Salem family.

Rev. E.P. Diggs then became pastor to serve for two years. Rev. S.J. Jones served after him from 1902-1907. These were busy years for Salem. The first Missionary Circle was organized, and a parsonage was purchased.

The next spiritual leader was Rev. J.C. Jackson who came from the pulpit of the historic Court Street Baptist Church of Lynchburg, Virginia. Under his leadership, Salem's first masonry church building was erected in 1909 replacing the old frame structure. Rev. Jackson served for seven years.

Salem then called Rev. Dr. J.A. Pinson in 1915. Dr. Pinson was instrumental in setting Salem on firm financial ground. The church saw enormous growth during his tenure. Dr. Pinson resigned the Salem pulpit in 1922. Rev. J.A. Jordan then became pastor and served until 1930. His leadership was marked by growth and development. The Church was remodeled and the first pipe organ was installed.

On the first Sunday of November 1931, Rev. William James Lucas became the next pastor of Salem. An erudite scholar, a unique preacher and a devoted servant of the people, Dr. Lucas had a long and distinguished pastorate at Salem. During his pastorate, the parsonage was remodeled, the side walls of the Church were rebuilt and the pipe organ was reconditioned. Several new organizations were begun by Pastor Lucas, including the Ever Ready Club and the Sunshine Chorus. In August 1955, after twenty-four years of devoted services to the Salem congregation, Dr. William James Lucas passed away.

Rev. George Watson, a son of Salem, became the itinerant pastor of Salem, serving during the fourteen difficult months after Dr. Lucas' death. In May of 1956, the Church extended the call to Rev. Robert Johnson-Smith, pastor of the Hill Street Baptist Church, Roanoke, Virginia. He began his pastorate in October 1956. The three churches Rev. Smith had served before coming to Salem had experienced unprecedented growth and development under his dynamic leadership. Rev. Smith had also served as a Chaplain, with the rank of Major, in the United States Army and at the Veterans' Administration Hospital in Roanoke, Virginia.

When Pastor Smith accepted the call of Salem in 1956*, he immediately began an in-depth study of the total needs of the congregation for that time and for the future. He noted that more space was needed to meet the needs of the youth, to become involved with the community, and to house the expanding congregation. Plans were made to enlarge and refurbish the church. The congregation worshipped at Beaver College during 1957 and 1958. Finally on Easter Sunday, March 29, 1959, after surmounting many difficulties, the Salem family was able to return to their Home Church.

In 1972, after years of struggle and frustrations, the Church completed construction of the Salem Baptist (SALBA) Apartments. Located at 309 Walnut Street, Jenkintown, the seventeen unit apartments are for low and middle income families. Special consideration for rentals is given to senior citizens. Under the direction of a non-profit organization, these apartments represent another part of the outreach of Salem and are viewed as a community service.

For many years the congregation saw the need for a place conducive for study and learning. For too long children, youths and adults had been cramped by limited space. On July 27, 1980, the Robert Johnson-Smith Education Center was dedicated and answered the longings and needs of the congregation. Today Rev. Catherine Godboldte works with Pastor Johnson-Smith as assistant pastor.

Any description of Salem Baptist Church must emphasize the story of the people of Salem for the church is entirely family centered, oriented around providing services that include all generations. Ex-slaves and free men gathered in this area after the Civil War, originally to provide domestic help for the wealthy. They came together to sing and pray and to testify to their personal relationship with God.

Sons and daughters of these ex-slaves became craftsmen, moving into industrial fields and working as carpenters, freemasons and jobbers. They gained more formal education than their parents and an improved economic status. Eventually, their children attended college and became members of all the professional fields. Throughout this progression the families remained in this area, maintaining church affiliation, and Salem became a focal point in their lives. These descendants of the original founders are augmented today by other families that live in many areas of Philadelphia. They are drawn to the warm family concept of the church.

The Salem of the future will be a fellowship of kindred souls linked with the wider fellowship of men and women of faith, reaching beyond the artificial barriers of race, color or creed. The Salem of the future will never forget its heritage. It will never forget the Founding Fathers, their faith, struggles, sorrows, failures, successes, poverty, prosperity as they lived and worked in the Church. We thank God for the legacy that is ours, and we are determined that we shall continue to live, work and serve "as People of God."

*Having served Salem and the wider Jenkintown community for thirty-four years, Rev. Johnson-Smith is the beloved and respected "dean" of the Jenkintown Ministerium. Modest about his accomplishments in the history above, he has earned the warm friendship and trust of such distinguished leaders as Rev. Martin Luther King, Jr., Congressman (Rev.) William Gray and other fighters for racial equality over the years of his exemplary ministry. He serves today as Chairman of the Pennsylvania State Human Relations Commission. [Editor]

*Simplicity is the keynote of this lovely church, warmed
by the red carpet and dossal curtain and by the oak of the pews and pulpit.*

Salem Baptist Church

TOUR

Enter the modern building of Salem Baptist and climb up a short flight of stairs to the sanctuary. At the rear of the church is the Martin Luther King Chapel. The doors of this chapel are usually closed unless additional seating is needed during the two Sunday services. However, the chapel is used for small prayer meetings, for weddings and for lectures. Two of Dr. King's famous quotations: *"I have a dream,"* and *"Free at last,"* hang on opposite walls. Three stained glass windows were recently installed into the west wall to depict the civil rights movement, including scenes from the bus boycott that was organized by Dr. King. Dr. King himself is the subject of the center window.

This martyred leader had close ties with Salem

Baptist, officiating at many church services. In fact, the stained glass window that hangs in the east wall of the church, visible when the dossal (curtain) is opened before each service to reveal the Baptismal area, was made possible by the generosity of Dr. King. Instead of taking an honorarium for lecturing at the church, he donated the money to the women of the congregation. This window, showing St. John baptizing Jesus, is the result of his gesture.

The long, narrow nave before you is really the original structure of the 1909 church which extends to the beginning of the transept. Even as the new church was being designed, the sense of history that surrounded the church remained. Members insisted

The Martin Luther King, Jr., Chapel and windows.

133

that the original structure be incorporated into the new building. There was an awareness of time, an understanding that parents and grandparents and all the many generations had prayed there. This continuity was to be treasured.

New stained glass windows were fashioned to fit the original spaces present in the old church. They match in pattern and feeling the older windows in the transept that date back to 1910. These are simple, but colorful windows that brightly transform the light entering into the church. All repeat the same basic form, with pillars framing the window's perimeter, rising to a pointed, architectural form. Within each is a symbol either of Christianity or of Old Testament roots set into the center of the window as a medallion. Moving counter-clockwise, beginning on the north wall are: Noah's ark, the dove, wheat stalks which, with the wine on the south wall, represent the Eucharist, and a flame to signify the light of faith.

The final window, closest to the west wall, is personally linked to the pastor of the church, Reverend Johnson-Smith. The medallion in the center of this window hints at tragedy. There are many stories in this church, many family histories revealed in the brass plaques that dot the chairs and the pews given in a person's memory or honor. This window was given in memory of Estelle Anne Smith, the Pastor's daughter. The modern insignia of Spelman College forms the window's medallion, the cross within making it a fitting sign for the church. "Our whole school for Christ," the motto proclaims. And there are the dates of Estelle's life: 1941-1966.

But the window cannot reveal the entire story. The Pastor was speaking at an intercongregational prayer service on that Good Friday. He later discovered that as he spoke Jesus' words: *"My Lord, why hast thou forsaken me?"* his family was involved in a car accident that killed his daughter. She was to have been married that summer and she was traveling home to finalize plans. Martin Luther King, Jr., had planned to officiate at her wedding. This window, with its modern feeling, at first seems markedly different from the others. But once the details are known, the tribute to Estelle Smith becomes one more in a church where a personal story becomes part of the entire church's history.

Note the simplicity of this church, warmed by the

The Estelle Anne Smith memorial window.

red carpet and the light oak used for the pews and for the pulpit that grows out of a half-wall separating the chancel from the nave. Walk towards the chancel and notice the very open feeling of the church at this point. This area, in which the choir sits, is most visible to the congregation.

Music plays an important part of the service in this church. There are several, separate choirs that fill the church with song. There are two youth choirs, one for teens and one for younger children, and there is an all male chorus that specializes in music suited for their voices. Two adult choirs also perform. One concentrates on traditional church music, the spirituals of slavery days that sing praise of God but also secretly express that desire for freedom. And there is a gospel choir that has won many prizes for excellence.

Pastor Smith's experience with gospel music dates back to the beginning of the tradition in the 1930s. At Ebenezer Baptist Church in Chicago where his father was pastor, individual singers like Mahalia Jackson, Roberta Martin and Theodore Frye came together to form choirs. The music gained momentum at that time and blossomed all over the country. This tradition grew from people who faced continuing hardships. The rhythms and the freedom of expression in the music is heart-felt. Gospel singing preceded the jazz movement which can trace its roots back to this tradition. Because of the musical diversity here, Salem Baptist has placed a concert piano, a pipe organ, and a more modern organ in the chancel.

Within the musical tradition are the historical roots of the prayer meeting that are still felt in today's service. In post-slavery days, small congregations were unable to afford hymnals for each member, some of whom were unable to read. "Lining the hymn," became the practice, where a soloist sang out each line and the congregation repeated in song. There was a responsiveness between congregation and leader that is continued in services at Salem Baptist. Individual responses are still encouraged. Notice the microphone placed before the pulpit at the front of the church. Here a lay person will lead the group in prayer, but still, from time to time, as in the prayer meeting, someone will rise during the service to bear witness, to relate a personal religious experience.

In addition to the prayer areas of Salem, there is the Robert Johnson-Smith Education Center, dedicated in 1980. It contains seven classrooms, utility rooms and offices for the Church School superintendant on the first level. The upper level contains the Irene Harling Board Room, the Trustees' Suite, a production room, a conference room, and the Pastor's Study.

Below the main church is the Lulu Price Dean Music Center, the home of the many Salem choirs, adult and youth. There are two rehearsal rooms, a music library, a robe room and an office for the Minister of Music. Also in this area is the Rev. Dr. W. J. Lucas Memorial Library with its excellent collection of works on black history as well as general religious reading material. An attractive Fellowship Hall provides space for dinners, meetings and recreational activities.

The church has grown to encompass the many religious and social needs of its community. But in spite of that growth, the past, viable and cherished, remains as motivation. The history of the church, which includes generations of the same families, has become a force in today's congregation, where people pray and sing in Christian fellowship, but where they are offered aid, support and guidance as well.

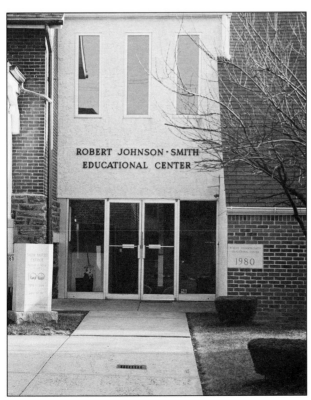

The Smith Educational Center.

Church of Our Saviour

Church of Our Saviour

Old York Road and Homestead Road, Jenkintown

HISTORY*

Beginning around 1845, attempts were made to establish an Episcopal church in Jenkintown by the Rev. George P. Hopkins, Rector of the St. Paul's Church, Doylestown, Pa., but without success. Then, in the 1850s, the North Penn Railroad made Jenkintown more accessible to the city. About this time and probably because of the railroad, some half dozen families who were desirous of the services of the Episcopal church moved to the area. They made application to the Rev. E.Y. Buchanan, Rector of Trinity Church, Oxford (a brother of the President of the United States) for services at the Jenkintown Lyceum during the summer months.

On August 29, 1855, there was a fatal railroad accident which was recorded by the Rev. Ormes B. Keith in his diary as follows: "Dreadful railroad accident occurred today just above Burlington, New Jersey. Upwards of 20 were killed and many severely wounded. Two members of the little congregation of the Jenkintown Lyceum, William Henry Newbold and his daughter, were in the accident." The former escaped without injury but the latter was so severely hurt that she was an invalid until her death.

Mr. Newbold refused to institute suit on behalf of either himself or his daughter which was in keeping with his character; however, the railroad voluntarily gave them $10,000 which the family devoted to the erecting of the church in Jenkintown as a thanks offering to Almighty God. Because of their miraculous escape, they decided upon the name "Church of Our Saviour." Placed over the door of the church facing York Road is the original bell from the train and the appropriate words from Psalm 68: "*God is the Lord by whom we escape death.*"

---

*We are grateful to Betty Helveston for preparing this history.

The minutes of the Vestry of July 6, 1858 read in part: "Church opened for divine services the 20th day of June. The sacrament was administered and collection taken." Mr. Ormes B. Keith, headmaster of a school connected with St. Mark's Church, Philadelphia, became first Rector of the Church of Our Saviour after entering the Holy Order. He was followed by the Rev. A. Francis Colton.

In 1888 Rev. Roberts Cole became the Rector. Under his tenure the transept was added, the low plaster ceiling in the nave was changed, and the organ was moved to a chamber on the south side of the chancel. The baptismal font was relocated near the south door, and the Vestry membership was increased from nine to twelve members. The envelope collection system of funds for the parish now allowed the church to be supported by the whole congregation and not by the generosity of a few. The boys' choir sang its first service on July 6, 1890. A choir room was opened in July 1895 as a memorial to Mrs. Charles Baeder.

Other improvements in 1897 included deepening the chancel twelve feet, a gift from Beauveau Borie, and rebuilding the organ chamber. In 1902 the Rectory was physically raised four feet to overcome the dampness within, and in 1906, an addition to the west end of the church was made. At this time the La Farge stained glass window was added.

As it entered the twentieth century, Church of Our Saviour addressed the spiritual welfare of outlying villages by establishing Parochial Missions. Thus the Church of Our Saviour became the mother church of the Chapel of All Hallows, Wyncote; St. Andrew's Mission, McKinley; another in Bethayres which would later be known as St. John's Huntingdon Valley; and a chapel in Willow Grove, later to become St. Anne's, Abington.

Further extensions of church grounds were made during successive years. A new Parish House was built in 1936 at the corner of Cottman Street on Homestead Road. Mrs. Henry G. Gibson donated the beautiful grandfather's clock and andirons in the common room.

During World War II, under the leadership of the Rev. Reginald Davis (Rector, 1933-1967), Our Saviour served the needs of servicemen by establishing "The Church Door Canteen" in the Parish House and offering socials, entertainment, and dances. The Canteen opened its doors in July 1943 with the cooperation of more than thirty community and religious organizations. During its first ten months, the canteen entertained over 11,000 servicemen. It was a community success with an international reputation.

As a result of the "baby boom" and the development of the area which occurred following the war, Our Saviour experienced a period of significant growth. "Reggie" Davis remained Rector until his death. In 1967 the Vestry called the Rev. Joseph Iredale to be Rector. As Mr. Davis' curate, "Joe" was well known to the Parish. Mr. Iredale, a native of White Plains, New York and graduate of the Philadelphia Divinity School, served as Rector until his untimely death in 1977. During his rectorship, Mr. Iredale emphasized the teaching and preaching ministry of the Church.

In November 1956, the new Rectory on Homestead Road was purchased. In 1960, it was resolved that two Vestry members should be women. The participation of women in the church service began in 1978 when one was named the first female acolyte. This was followed by two others who were certified as lay readers.

The Women's Auxiliary and the Parish Guild merged to become the Auxiliary Guild, the forerunner of Episcopal Churchwomen, that name being used for the first time in 1960. The Churchwomen raise money for the support of missions and contribute to the General Fund of the Church.

The late '70s and early '80s were a period of transition and controversy in the Episcopal Church. The Rev. Richard Risser, who succeeded Mr. Iredale as Rector (1977-1983), guided the congregation through the introduction of the newly revised *Book of Common Prayer*. Fr. Risser, a native of Allentown and graduate of Bexley Hall in Rochester, introduced several liturgical innovations including the free-standing altar. The changing community was reflected in Our Saviour's congregation as most of the old established families moved elsewhere and newer, younger families moved in. As a result, Our Saviour today reflects a more diverse and "ecumenical" congregation.

Several organizations have started in the past twenty-five years. One is the Seabury Society whose purpose is to strengthen fellowship through social activities. Another organization is a prayer group, organized in 1979, which brings to those who are ill or troubled the comfort and prayerful support of fellow members of the congregation. "The Corner," the church's own Thrift Shop, was started in 1978. In 1982, Vacation Bible School was first held at the church, providing the children of the parish and the community at large with five nights of Bible stories, music, crafts and games.

During the rectorship of the Rev. Dr. Kenneth J. Wissler (1985-), Our Saviour has continued to minister to the needs and concerns of a community and congregation which has changed much during the past two decades. Dr. Wissler, a native of Wilmington, Delaware, received his doctorate from Fuller Theological Seminary in Pasadena, California. While building on the traditions of the past, Our Saviour continues to meet the spiritual needs of a changing community.

One of the interesting innovations of the last few years is the use of our church on Sunday afternoons for worship services of the Hap Dong Korean Presbyterian Church. That the Church of Our Saviour has helped to foster and shelter this Christian congregation has been a source of great satisfaction.

*Dark woods, brass pulpit and lectern, baptismal font, and
chancel — all fix the attention of the worshiper in this "English country church."*

Church of Our Saviour

TOUR

The origin of the Church of Our Saviour as a place where thanks may be offered to God is immediately apparent to the visitor. Etched in stone around the peak of the welcoming red wooden door is the inscription: *"God is the Lord by whom we escape death."* This is the first reference to the Newbold family, patrons of the growing church community. Thankful for life after a terrible train accident in 1855, the family donated the insurance money paid to them by the railroad to build the church that was completed in

1858. Above the red door hangs the original bell from the train. Inside the stone building, memorials to the Newbolds are found in plaques as well as on several stained glass windows.

The elements of an English country church are easily recognized in the nave of this church. The interior is filled with dark wood and white-washed walls. Paneled wainscoting meets the walls, and the warm wood of the arched roof, with its hammerhead, wooden trusses, lifts the eye upward. Above the many stained glass windows that cut the white walls with a myriad of colors is the unusual, but beautiful addition of painted frescos. Added in the early 1970s, the frescos flow around the church directly below the roof line as the soft browns and beiges of the flowering vines blend with the warmth of the wood throughout.

Framing each window are different frescos that gently outline the depth of the windows but do not conflict with the beauty of the stained glass. All of the windows are treated in the same fashion. The effect is of the traditional church, where the atmosphere has been warmed by a modern use of an ancient form of church decoration.

In the nave, one window stands apart from the others. Situated on the north wall, second from the west end door, is a large stained glass window, executed by the La Farge Studios, in memory of Mary Scott Newbold after her death in 1905. The style here is reminiscent of Tiffany windows of the same period. Layers of glass have been applied, producing some extraordinary effects of color that are not merely brilliant, but also show great depth as in the wings and in the clothing of the figures. In this window, an angel of adoration kneels before the young Jesus. The young man holds a book on which Hebrew letters are printed. The window portrays the calling of Christ before the word became flesh, in a sense, Christ before the

The welcoming red wood door.

Windows framed by frescos.

is the kingdom of heaven."

Notice the abundant use of brass in front of the chancel. To the left is the pulpit, set off from the white walls by the intricate brass work that is open and lacy in feeling. Woven into the design is the traditional cross with the *IHS* symbol that dates from the time of Constantine, the first Christian Emperor. Tradition says that Constantine dreamed of victory in battle because of his faith in God. Thus, *"In Hoc Signo* — in this sign [you will prevail]", was emblazoned into the Romans' shields.

Behind the pulpit is the brass rood screen, gothic in feeling, that sets off, but does not obscure, the altar from view. On the right of the screen is an intricately designed brass lectern, given, in 1881, in memory of the second church rector, Richard Francis Colton. The eagle in ancient times was considered the highest flying bird, one that could fly closest to the sun and therefore closest to God. The bird represents man's spiritual aspirations, or the word of God pulling man heavenward.

Walk towards the north transept wall to view the three stained glass windows there. The large central window depicts the Pentecost, after Christ's Ascension. Here the disciples and some women followers are gathered in the upper room where the Last Supper took place. While at prayer, the Holy Spirit descended upon them, evidenced here by the bright red flame that burns above their heads. Notice the oddly colored faces of the disciples. While the faces are realistically portrayed, the skin tones are grey, brown, purple and blue. Only St. Peter, standing before a kneeling Virgin Mary, is portrayed naturally. Perhaps the artist mean to suggest the mission of the church to preach the gospel to peoples of all races, and to realize the universality of Jesus' message.

Above the gathered figures St. John baptises Jesus. Hovering over the two is a small gray dove, reminding the viewer that the Holy Spirit descended upon Jesus like a dove.

To either side of this large window, the two smaller windows depict the healing ministry of Jesus. On the right, Jesus raises Jairus' daughter. On the left, Jesus heals the woman with the hemorrhage. Notice the use of borders in the three windows, intricately designed to set off the various scenes without interfering with their power. Also note the use of architectural

nativity. The figures are bordered by details resembling architecture. As the sky glows behind them, the figure of Christ is highlighted, His face and body bathed in light.

Walk down the nave towards the chancel. Pause as you reach the point where the transept stretches to the right and the left. Turn towards the south wall to notice a round stained glass window above the door. This the second round window in the church; the first is above the west end door. Here, the traditional symbol of the Holy Spirit soars as the dove's white wings and body fill the small window. Beams of light radiate outward, suggesting the encompassing power of the Spirit. The dove hangs in the blue space, spreading its wings to enfold all who worship there.

In front of the chancel is the baptismal font that was donated in 1866 by Mary Newbold Singer, grandmother of the artist, John Singer Sargent. Appropriate words encircle the marble basin: *"Suffer little children to come unto Me and forbid them not, for of such*

Center: the Pentecost; Right and left: Jesus' healing ministry.

details, the church spires on the top, the fabric screen in the right window, the narrowing floor tiles in the central one, all producing a feeling of depth or perspective in the scene.

Turn now and enter the chancel, passing beneath the small blue crosses that fill a fresco bordering the opening arch. Directly in front of the brass altar rail are floor tiles filled with Christian symbols, reminiscent of the use of mosaics in ancient churches. Intricate, needlepointed kneeling cushions, executed recently by a local pediatrician, Dr. Richard Ellison, line the altar rail.

Behind the marble altar, three large windows in memory of John Newbold throw light on the place of Communion. Geometric in design, vibrant bands of colors intersect in these windows added in 1897. Depicted are Christian symbols, the cross with its interwoven letters and the grape vine that represents both the Eucharist and Jesus. Within the windows, bold medallions in bursts of solid color are set at intervals.

The Church of Our Saviour is filled with the memories of the Newbolds and many other early families that founded it. Within its walls are over a hundred years of history. Rich in the symbolism of Christianity, the church holds many decorative elements that add dimension and warmth to the interior. But the church's design is not static, not fixed in the past. New additions such as the unusual frescos and the rich needlepoint testify to the ongoing committment of the church members.

Within the building are other activities that take place, reflecting a changing community. A Korean Presbyterian congregation that is without its own meeting place has been welcomed. They hold their own worship services in the church. The Parish House behind the church hosts meetings of diverse local groups, ranging from a well-baby clinic and the Cubscouts to the American Association of Retired Persons. Founded when Jenkintown was new, The Church of Our Saviour continues to offer a place for gathering as well as a home for worship.

Grace Presbyterian Church

Grace Presbyterian Church

Old York Road and Vista Road, Jenkintown

HISTORY

The Presbyterian Church (USA) is a church of both order and ardor. Its order comes through the structures which have been established in the courts of church government so that the faithful may properly serve and express the will of God. Its ardor comes from the zeal with which issues of both piety and justice are pursued. Grace Presbyterian Church of Jenkintown is a direct result of such a heritage.

Grace Church began because of the ardor of three men: the Rev. Robert Steele, pastor of Abington Presbyterian Church (1819-1862); his successor, the Rev. Samuel T. Lowrie; and Mr. John Wanamaker, a prominent Philadelphia resident and businessman and an active Presbyterian layman.

In 1845 the Rev. Robert Steele began holding prayer services once a month in the Jenkin's Town Lyceum, the building which now houses the Jenkintown Library. Connected with these services was a Sunday School for the instruction of youth in the Jenkintown area. However, as Pastor Steele's health failed, the services were discontinued, and the Sunday School was taken over by the Episcopal Church.

Under the leadership of a new pastor at Abington Presbyterian, the Rev. Samuel T. Lowrie, it was ascertained that there were twenty-six families in his church who were residents of Jenkintown; there was need for a school for the religious instruction of their children near their homes. And so a new Presbyterian Sabbath School was formed in the Lyceum which quickly grew to the point where it required a building of its own.

It was at this time that John Wanamaker, an active layman at Tenth Presbyterian Church in Philadelphia whose summer residence was in Jenkintown, approached Pastor Lowrie with a proposal. If the Abington Church would provide the lot on York Road, Wanamaker would construct a building suit-

able for a Sabbath School. The lot was purchased from the Lyceum in 1870, and a building large enough for instruction and suitable for church services was completed in September, 1872. On September 8, 1872 John Wanamaker himself led a procession of 165 persons out of the Lyceum and across the street to the newly completed facility called "Grace Chapel."

The ardor of three men to establish a Sunday School for children was blessed with continuing growth. By 1881 it was clear that a new church, to correspond with the new Borough of Jenkintown (1874), was in order. The Presbytery of Philadelphia concurred and ordered that the new Grace Presbyterian Church of Jenkintown be commissioned on May 6, 1881.

The name of the church is taken from the New Testament passage of scripture in Ephesians: *"For by grace have you been saved through faith."* The emphasis of the church from its inception has been the nurturing of God's grace in the life of the faithful through worship and instruction.

The campus of Grace Presbyterian Church has changed several times since its founding in 1881. The original Victorian structure which housed the Sunday School building is still used today. It was remodeled in 1956 to include two rooms: Wanamaker Chapel, which is the room where John Wanamaker used to visit with the church school children after he had built the building, and the Palmer Room, which houses the Cecil Harding Jones Library and also serves as the church's parlor. The Palmer Room is named after the wife of one of the former pastors who was a prominent Bible teacher during her husband's tenure, and the Jones Library is named for the pastor under whose leadership the church saw its greatest growth.

The current sanctuary of the church is not the

original building which housed its worship. As the church grew in membership, the original building was expanded in 1907 to enlarge the seating in the chancel area by sixty per cent. As the need for Sunday School and office space grew, the church responded by erecting the educational wing of the building in 1927. The current sanctuary and the educational facilities in the basement beneath the sanctuary were built in 1956 during a period of rapid growth in the congregation's membership. However, in order to maintain continuity with the church's past, the wall of the south transept was maintained along with some of the original stained glass so that the historical link to the roots of the church would be complete.

The present campus includes a play yard on Vista Rd., and the church manse (pastor's residence) at the corner of Vernon and Vista Rds. The play yard serves the Grace Nursery School, which was established in 1952 to be a community outreach, and has served the community continuously for thirty-six years.

Ten pastors have served the church since its establishment in 1881. They are: The Rev. Henry A. McKubbin (1882-1886); The Rev. Richard Greene (1886-1894); The Rev. John M. Stephens (1895-1902); The Rev. Edward Riley (1903-1905); The Rev. William K. Foster (1906-1920); The Rev. Francis Palmer (1922-1928); The Rev. Dr. John Muyskens (1930-1948); The Rev. Cecil Jones (1948-1973); The Rev. William J. Murphey (1974-1983); and The Rev. Dr. Randolph T. Riggs (1984-present). In addition, the church has been served by several assistant pastors, as well as the significant contribution of a Commissioned Church Worker for thirty-three years (1952-1985), Miss Helen Fields.

Each of these church leaders has brought his own unique contribution to the life and ministry of the congregation. Under their guidance the church has become noted for its excellence in music, preaching, Christian education, and community service.

At its peak the membership of Grace Church reached nearly 1800. Active membership in the Presbyterian church requires regular participation in church worship, church programs and some indica-

tion of financial support. Since the late 1960s, with the secularization of our society and the changes in demographics in Jenkintown and surrounding communities, membership has declined to 730 members.

However, those who remain and those who have recently joined remain committed to the ideals of the church which have made it a strong witness since those early days as a mission Sunday School. There continues to be a vital program of Christian Education for children and youth; programs of adult nurture and spiritual growth; a vibrant worship service with excellent music and vital preaching; and newly organized programs of service to the community which include concern for those addicted to drugs and alcohol and for the homeless, plus Jewish/Christian as well as Black/White dialogues intended to overcome racism and prejudice.

Openness to the future has been demonstrated most recently in 1984 with the purchase of the property adjacent to the Grace campus. This property has served the community for over 50 years, first as a Thriftway Market and then T-Bird Bowling Lanes. It was originally the site of the Jenkins estate.

After considerable discussion as to the future of the property, the congregation voted to sell it to one of its members for purposes of development as a personal care facility for the elderly. Recognizing the need for such a facility and the lack of financial resources of the church to complete the construction, the decision was made not to be selfish but to sell the property so that it might serve the community.

At the dedication of the new buildings of Grace in April, 1956, Dr. Paul Payne set forth a challenge which Grace Church has continued to use as its hallmark: "What will (the future) bring and what will Grace Church do in such a situation? I think I know the answer to that question, the way the future will go. The future will go to those who care most."

Thus, as it looks to the future, Grace Presbyterian Church strives to be a church where both its members and the community experience the caring presence of a loving God.

"And the Word was made flesh" is the proclamation
of the intricate, five-panel window that admits light to the Chancel.

Grace Presbyterian Church

TOUR

It was the Jenkin Town Lyceum, now used as the Jenkintown Library, that housed the small group of Presbyterians in the early days of the Grace Church. In 1845 a Sunday school offered instruction to the children of people who were continuing to worship at the Abington Presbyterian Church. But it was not until 1872 that an independent building was erected to house the growing church community.

The moving force behind building a chapel that would continue Sunday morning lessons was John Wanamaker, who became a benefactor of the new church. The chapel housed at Grace Presbyterian still bears his name. He taught one of the first Bible lessons in the new Grace Chapel in 1872.

The exterior of the chapel is what remains of the original church buildings. A larger church was built in the early 1880s after the church had been officially established in 1881 as independent from Abington Presbyterian. That building was used until 1955 when a decision was made to enlarge the physical facilities because of the growing church family. While some of the other buildings remain from that early period, the original church was torn down then and the current church was erected on the same location.

The new church would seat over 500 worshippers and provide an enlarged choir area as well as a social room and classrooms for study. A modified Gothic style was chosen to blend the new church with the remaining buildings. Rising forty-six feet above the church is an elongated spire that announces the church's presence even before it can be viewed from the street.

Inscribed above the main entrance are the words: *"For By Grace Are We Saved Through Faith,"* proclaiming the orientation of the church. Within the narthex are windows originally hung in the walls of the 1881 church. These windows, marked with the names of those memorialized there, had hung in various locations scattered throughout the old church. Now they are placed side by side, still in remembrance of the early church members.

A feeling of volume and size is most apparent as you enter the nave. Wooden wainscotting, wooden beams crisscrossing the ceiling that rises in the strong pitch of Gothic churches and white walls surrounding the wooden pews, all produce a simple interior where most of the decorative details have been reserved for the intricate stained glass windows.

Main entrance with Grace inscription.

Window from original church, dedicated to memory of Pastor Stephens.

The south transept which is situated towards the west wall, contains a window from the original church. Because of this window dedicated to Reverend John M. Stephens, pastor of the church from 1895-1902, the wall in which it hangs was the only wall not torn down. This window is markedly different from the other windows in the church, presenting a single, simple image of Christ, standing among the clouds of heaven. All the stained glass, with the exception of the memorial window in the Chancel, were produced by Willet Studio in the mid-1950s when the new church was designed.

The other stained glass windows depict the story of the life of Jesus, beginning with His birth, which is the subject of the large Chancel window. The details of His life follow in a counter-clockwise fashion continuing with the windows on the north wall. The story ends with the Ascension shown on the south wall just before the memorial window. The final window on this side portrays the gospel of Jesus,

showing Paul preaching at Athens, Christian Martyrs, and Missionaries, all elements of the Christian Church.

These smaller windows, made up of two panels or lancets, are quite intricate in design. They are filled with a multitude of detail and color, peopled with the many characters in the life of Christ. But recognizable within each is Jesus who wears the same robes and gazes outward with the same face. Because of His presence there is unity in the windows.

In the north transept, a triple window shows the miracles of Jesus. The strong vertical sense of the windows is repeated here so that the story can be read from top to bottom. On the left Jesus heals the lepers, raises Lazarus from the dead, and heals a lone leper. In the middle there is the miracle of the Feeding of the Five Thousand. Below this is Christ healing the sick, and then the Centurion thanking Jesus for healing his slave. On the right Jesus walks on water and raises Jairus's daughter from the dead. Finally the Carmelite woman, whose daughter Jesus has cured, appears.

It is the window in the Chancel that makes one of the strongest visual statements of the church. The scene was fashioned in 1914 by Heaton, Butler, and Bayne, a famous stained glass firm. It originally hung in the Protestant Episcopal Church of the Incarnation in Philadelphia. Many years after being removed from this church and many years after being boxed and stored, it was given to Grace by Mr. and Mrs. Herbert L. Phillips of Langhorne. James Evans Mitchell, Mrs. Philips maternal grandfather, had commissioned the window in memory of his wife, Sarah Jane Mitchell.

While as intricate as the other glass in the church, all panels of this window come together to form a unified portrait, to capture one moment in Jesus' early life. Mary sits in the center of the window, elevated on an earthly throne, the apex of a triangle of figures that surround her. She seems serene as she gazes down at the Infant in her lap. Jesus rests there against His mother, but gazes outward, reaching with arms towards the men who have come to worship.

Joseph stands on the left, with one arm drawing the shepherds next to him into the scene, and with the other arm pointing towards the Infant Jesus. On the right side are the wise men. Each of the scene's participants has weight and volume, with the folds of fabric draping around very realistic bodies. There is such attention given to realism that even their hands have been modeled, tendons and fingers given in such detail that the total effect is to transform the figures in the glass into almost living shapes.

In the lower part of the window are symbols which enhance the story being told. Below Mary and Jesus, the mother sheep and baby lamb rest side by side. Included also are other details: the sheaf of wheat, the lily, the thistle, the lily of the valley, and the doves. Two more doves sit on top of the rustic building above Mary.

Perhaps it is color that sets this window off from the others. A delicate tinge of green dominates. Shades of green have become the neutral color here, warmed by rich reds and purples and given depth by the cool blues all used in the rich robes of the participants in the scene. Brown is used abundantly to depict the building and the trees behind the figures. Deep in the background sky, the Star of Bethlehem shines in the night. In the upper window, angels and cherubim appear, linking heaven with the events of earth. The words *"and the Word was made flesh,"* are proclaimed

on a scroll unfurled above the earthly scene.

Opposite this powerful scene in the chancel is a small window that seems to burn into the west wall. Like a flower, the rose window is filled with the deepest, richest colors, intensifying those colors found in the windows. The petals radiate outward from the center. Filled with symbols that tell of the suffering of Jesus and also with symbols that depict the twelve Apostles, all that really can be seen from the nave is color. Given in memory of Lulu M. Bowles, the window captures as much attention as does the powerful scene in the chancel.

Even though this is a recent building filled with the beauty of the stained glass, the roots of the early congregation have not been forgotten. Visit the John Wanamaker Chapel to view a window that memorializes its benefactor. The chapel was refurbished in a colonial style when the church was rebuilt in 1955. A window was then commissioned from Ralph Pallen Coleman to honor Wanamaker's contribution. Wanamaker's portrait is the focal point of the window. He is surrounded by worthy details of his life: the Bible which he taught on so many Sunday mornings; the seal of the Postmaster General, a position he held

Narthex windows from original church.

in 1889 on the bottom left, and the seal of the Young Men's Christian Association, which he served as secretary, on the right. Behind him rise the Wanamaker center city building and the tower of City Hall.

The window in the rear of the Chapel was also designed by Coleman, who often tried to link history and faith to present day events. Here the left panel is in tribute to the fallen of World War II, while the right panel reaches back to the beginnings of the country by depicting George Washington at Valley Forge. But it is the center two panels that reveal Coleman's philosophy. Next to the soldier, Moses as representative of the Old Testament, stands beside Jesus in the other panel. The designer's message is clear: faith fashioned so long ago continues in the present, offering strength to those who must serve.

Old York Road Temple Beth Am

Old York Road Temple Beth Am

971 Old York Road, Abington

HISTORY

Abington's Old York Road Temple Beth Am is a pioneering Liberal-Reform Synagogue. Affiliated with the Federation of Reform Synagogues of Greater Philadelphia and the Union of American Hebrew Congregations, its Liberal-Reform orientation is evident in its optional use of the traditional Jewish head-covering (*kipah*) and prayer shawl (*tallit*) along with the Reform liturgy.

Temple Beth Am is the only synagogue along York Road that has its roots in this area. Unlike the others, Beth Am did not begin in Philadelphia to move here later along with the waves of Jewish population. Rather the congregation is a relatively new one that grew from the post-World War II days.

The congregation came into being in 1946 when some fifty or sixty families formed the Old York Road Jewish Community Center. From 1947 to 1951 the congregation functioned for the most part in the old Ehrenport building of Willow Grove (above a drug store). Its first High Holy Day services were held at the Abington YMCA and then, in later years, at the Curtis Arboretum in Wyncote. Members still remember the homemade portable Ark that had to be carried to the Arboretum for each service.

In 1950, the congregation changed its name to Old York Road Temple and acquired as a permanent home the McNair/Merritt Mansion on Noble Hill, originally built in 1825 and later used as a boarding school. This home became Beth Am, "The House of the People," in 1959 when the Frank Strick Auditorium and the Religious School was attached to it. These buildings were completed and dedicated in 1959.

A new central structure was planned to replace the old mansion building and to connect with the Strick Auditorium and the School Building to form an integrated complex. The conception of the total

building was that of the noted architect, Vincent G. Kling. Construction began in 1970 and was completed in 1972. The new edifice includes a Chapel, office complex, and new Sanctuary. The latter, dedicated in 1975 by Theodore and David Molish in loving memory of their parents, is a warm and peaceful place, whose physical presence provides a calm atmosphere and creates a contemplative mood for those who meet within its walls.

Rabbi Harold B. Waintrup was called to be Beth Am's first full-time Rabbi in 1951, and he is now in his thirty-ninth year at the Synagogue. He officiated at the dedication of the Chapel, Ark and Pulpit, with a congregation, at that time, of less than one hundred. He has served as a member of the Executive Board of the Central Conference of American Rabbis, and, in the past, has been president of the Eastern Montgomery County Ministers' Association and the Board of Rabbis of Greater Philadelphia.

In its forty-four-year history the Synagogue has had eighteen presidents, four part-time or assistant Rabbis and four Cantors. The Synagogue now has some 800 families and about 500 children in its Religious School, with a faculty of forty. The Assistant Rabbi is Robert S. Leib; the Principal is Arthur Beyer; and the Executive Director of Synagogue since 1980 is Marcia Goldman.

Old York Road Temple-Beth Am's early motto was "big enough to serve, small enough to know you." Our leadership, lay and spiritual, runs the Synagogue in the spirit of democracy. It has been said that the Rabbi's role at Beth Am has been one of "a co-creator of the Temple, in genuine partnership with the laity. Accordingly [the Rabbi] practices a congregational relationship based on reciprocal action and reaction."

Intimacy is perhaps a fitting word to describe this

congregation. The synagogue sponsors many activities that welcome the individual to share common goals. Beth Am is active in collecting food for the Jewish poor and works hard on behalf of Soviet Jewry. Beth Am has a program of "twinning" which links the Bar or Bat Mitzvah students with Soviet Jewish children and now also with Ethiopian Jewish children. The Scholar-in-Residence Program brings an artist or musician to further enrich the members' lives.

A full and active program of spiritual, social and educational programs has been part and parcel of Beth Am's dynamic growth. The Synagogue's goal has been to enrich the lives of congregants with the beauty of the Jewish tradition, and to blend into everyday life the teachings of the Liberal Reform tradition.

*The modern design of the bold stained glass and
brass Ark stands out like a flame from the surrounding brick walls.*

Old York Road Temple Beth Am

TOUR

The Temple Beth Am building is modern, consisting of three individual areas that interlock to function as a cohesive whole. In the center is the Molish Building where the Sanctuary is situated. To the left is the Frank Strick Auditorium that serves as a social hall; to the right is the wing that holds the class rooms of the religious schools.

Enter the Molish building to stand in a multi-leveled foyer. This area, like the other major parts of the synagogue, utilizes the same building materials. The warmth of red brick paves the floors in a herringbone design. The same brick forms the walls of the irregularly shaped rooms, for the major areas of the synagogue are triangles, brick-filled wedges of a large circle that has been divided and subdivided into interesting spaces.

The wall facing the entrance appears to be made entirely of glass. In fact the effect, as you stand in the downstairs foyer, is a pleasant experience of greenery as the abundance of indoor plants links one with the garden, viewed through the glass wall beyond. This garden, which is used when weather permits, is formed by the two wings of the building that come together at a sharp angle here.

Steps lead downstairs to what has been called the "garden room." Here small receptions, Oneg Shabbats, and meetings, such as the Singles Group, are held. To the right is the Klein Chapel. The brick floor and concrete walls lend a sculpturesque quality to the room that is shaped like a rounded triangle. Israeli woven wall tapestries that illustrate Bible stories hang along the walls. Here the *Ner Tamid* looks like

The courtyard garden.

163

a flame captured in burning red glass and hangs above an Ark that continues the sculpture of the room. The slabs of the Ten Commandments and the scroll of the Torah adorn the Ark doors, three-dimensional in simulated stone.

Upstairs is the Schulhoff Lounge where members of the congregation come together in the family atmosphere that is the orientation of this synagogue. Against the red brick walls spirals the Tree of Life. This congregation records *simchahs* or happy occasions: births, Bar and Bat Mitzvahs, milestone anniversaries, and good deeds, by adding leaves to the Tree. The limbs curl upwards in a darkened bronze. Adorning each branch is a leaf that is composed of small disks engraved with the event honored. The disks glitter against the red walls and from the dark branches in a polished brass that stand out dramatically. Here the congregation collects the happy moments of the extended family. From the large window here the 1972 cornerstone, containing memorabilia of the synagogue, can be seen. It has been symbolically placed directly below the Ark of the Main Sanctuary.

Through the glass doors ahead is the Main Sanctuary. On the wall directly opposite the doors is the Sherman Yahrzeit Wall. The area is illuminated in remembrance of the Six Million who perished during the Holocaust and in memory of the Israeli soldiers who died during the Yom Kippur War. Stained glass rectangles, like fragile scrolls, hang next to each other, symbolically containing names of the dead. Here too, individual members of the synagogue who have passed on are remembered. On the anniversary of each person's death, a brass plaque bearing that person's name is added to the wall. Just as the Tree of Life commemorates happiness, the Wall here acknowledges the end of the life cycle and focuses on the greatest tragedy of the twentieth century as well.

The Main Sanctuary is a dramatic room, structured with a soaring ceiling, the continuing brick walls, and the warm gold of the carpeting meant to represent desert sands. Like the smaller Chapel, the Main Sanctuary is also a triangle whose outer walls are rounded. The congregation sits in the warmth of a semicircle, facing the *bima*, here treated like a rounded platform that rises gently from the downward sloping floor. The *bima* is separated from the congregation, but appears a natural extension of the rest of the room.

In this Sanctuary, the placement of the *Ner Tamid* and the Ark is somewhat different from the traditional locations of both. The Ark, designed and executed by Marko Zubar, is nestled into the apex of the triangle. Like a free-standing unit, it is fashioned

Holocaust Memorial and Yahrzeit Wall.

entirely of brass and stained glass. The modern treatment is not sterile or cold. Rather the brilliant colors, the oranges, yellows, and reds, fashioned in an upward angled design, seem to burn against the brick and the glass wall behind it. The Ark glows through this window, allowing those in the garden room and even in the Klein Chapel to glimpse the burning colors.

To the front of the *bima*, the *Ner Tamid* hangs at the lowest point of the ceiling. Again made of brass and glass, the Eternal Light glimmers in the suggestion of a multitude of colors. The light is represented by glass, cut into flame-like shapes, that irregularly jut out of the brass casement. The flames of this Eternal Light remind the worshipper of the story of Moses, as God revealed His presence to the prophet through the unconsumed Burning Bush.

Above the *Ner Tamid*, the Star of David is etched into the concrete ceiling. Other stars grow from this initial one, building the image of a pulsing symbol of the Jewish faith. The movement begun here is continued by the dramatic ceiling that radiates outward from this point. Beams reach high into the sky, lifting the roof line and ending near the string of clerestory windows that follows the outside edge of the circle. Fan-like, the rays push outwards from the pulpit where God's words are read and reach towards the heavens. The rays are reminiscent of the rabbi's hands as he raises them, fingers spread, invoking God's love in blessing the congregation. On the other side of the *Ner Tamid*, the rays move towards the Ark and are separated by translucent glass of angled windows set into the ceiling.

On either side of the *bima* are two modern Menorahs that are almost woven into the structure of the walls. The elongated simple brass forms extend in a sharply horizontal fashion. Brick "arms" capture the flames of each limb.

Wood is another material utilized here. High on the right wall, the choir loft is separated from view by a wooden, slatted curtain. Music filters to the worshippers without the presence of the choir as a distraction. The lecterns on the *bima* are built in a similar fashion, faced with slats of wood that add dimension to the rectangular shapes.

The Main Sanctuary of Beth Am is one of dramatic simplicity. The beauty of the craftsmanship seen in the Ark and the Eternal Light, the drama of the roof line, the warmth of the natural materials used, all contribute to an intimate atmosphere in which to worship.

Beth Am, while growing, continues to encourage the intimacy suggested by the building itself, welcoming each worshipper into a larger family to join a dynamic Jewish tradition.

The Main Sanctuary.

Abington Presbyterian Church

Abington Presbyterian Church

Old York Road and Susquehanna Road, Abington

HISTORY*

Originally, Old York Road was the result of a petition made in 1693 by settlers in Cheltenham for a road. In 1697 the road from Susquehanna Street to Moreland Road in Willow Grove was laid out. Not until 1711 was York Road extended to the Delaware River in Bucks County to become the main road from Philadelphia to New York. Susquehanna Street Road (the early and official name) was one of the first roads laid out in Penn's land grant, and early deeds, prior to 1695, show that the road was used as a center or dividing line for making surveys.

In this newly developing area, Abington Presbyterian Church was founded in 1714, sixty-two years before the signing of the Declaration of Independence. It is the third oldest Presbyterian church in the Commonwealth of Pennsylvania. Benjamin Franklin was still a child and George Washington, Thomas Jefferson and John Adams had not yet been born when seventy hearty pioneers banded together in a primitive settlement to unite in the worship of God.

For their leader and pastor they selected Rev. Malachi Jones, then sixty-three years of age. It was in his home on the east side of York Road that seventy people adopted and signed their Covenant.

This small congregation held its services there until 1719 when Mr. Jones sold one-half acre of his farm to the trustees "to build a House for the Public Worship of God ... And also a place for Burying the Dead." Work on the log church began at once. It was located in the center of the Burying Ground, known as the Abington Cemetery today.

Malachi Jones served the church for fifteen years, and it was well established by the time of his death on

*Based on information taken from a pamphlet compiled by Walter and Doris Lufkin.

March 26, 1729. He is buried in the church cemetery. His will is in the church historical collection. A church deed, signed by Benjamin Franklin, is also among the collection.

When the Rev. Richard Treat was installed as the second pastor in 1731, the ordination sermon preached by the fiery Welsh preacher, David Evans, was published by Benjamin Franklin. The ministry of Richard Treat was to last forty-seven years, the longest pastorate in the church's history.

These were eventful years not only for Abington Church, but also for the emerging nation. During the days when Philadelphia was occupied by the British, the American Army marched through Abington several times and part of the Army was stationed here. British soldiers, camped in Philadelphia, made frequent raids into the country. On at least one such occasion, the British marched up York Road toward Abington only to be repulsed by American soldiers entrenched behind the wall of Abington Cemetery.

In 1756, when the Church was struggling for survival, one hundred acres of land on the west side of York Road were donated to the church. This was used as a church farm, rental fees from which helped support the church for the next hundred years.

On this newly acquired land was built the first manse which was to serve Abington pastors until its sale with the church farm in 1856. Although there have been several renovations, the original manse still stands. It is the large stone house at the corner of York and Orchard Roads.

By the time the war hostilities ended, the devastation of the Revolution and the widespread poverty and distress had so depleted both the membership and revenue of the church that it was practically disorganized. New life was breathed into the church, however, under the dynamic leadership of Rev. William Tennent, accompanied by the national surge of reconstruction after the war. It was time for a new church, this time on the west side of York Road. The old building in the cemetery was dismantled, and nothing of it exists today.

This new church, built in 1793, was to stand for forty years until the now thriving congregation required an even larger building. Stone from the original building was used to erect the new church. Services began in the morning and lasted until two in the afternoon.

When Abington's fifth pastor died in 1862, he was buried near the pastors who preceded him. The first five pastors who served this church for a total of 148 years, all died in its service and are buried side by side in Abington Church Cemetery.

Near the end of the Civil War, John Wanamaker purchased a home in Jenkintown and became active in the spiritual life of the community. It was he who brought to Abington some of its more distinguished visitors, among them evangelist Dwight L. Moody and U.S. President Benjamin Harrison.

At the end of the nineteenth century, surrounded by growth, Abington Church soon needed increased space and had just completed major expansions when disaster struck. At three o'clock on the morning of October 6, 1895, a motorman making a night run on the York Road trolley saw the red glow of fire. He awakened the pastor. Despite the heroic efforts of Rev. Henderson and Capt. Nicholas Baggs, the flames finally reached the steeple and the well-known landmark crashed to the ground. Within a year the church was rebuilt and John Wanamaker donated a new bell

for the steeple. The bell hangs there to this day.

In contrast to the years of growth, the dawn of the twentieth century saw Abington Presbyterian Church in a period of decline. However, elaborate plans were made to celebrate the 200th anniversary in 1914. From that time forward, membership continued to grow, necessitating additions and alterations to the church buildings.

Abington Church is the mother church, both directly and indirectly, of ten offspring churches in the area, among them Grace Church in Jenkintown, Carmel Church in Glenside, and Huntingdon Valley Presbyterian Church.

Rev. Robert M. Hoag was named Senior Pastor of the Church in 1975. Under his leadership many new programs were instituted, including a chapter of Compassionate Friends (parents who have lost children), an Abington community Thanksgiving Service, "We Can Say No" (an anti-drug program), a new ministry to older adults, a food delivery service to shut-ins called "Aid for Friends," the adoption of a family of Laotian "boat people," and many others. Rev. Hoag retired from his devoted fourteen-year ministry in June, 1989. As we go to press, an interim pastor, Fred Swearingen, is serving the Church.

Mr. Stanley Powell has served as Minister of Music since 1970 and has organized an ambitious program including sacred music concerts open to the public.

Abington Presbyterian Church celebrated its 275th year of service in 1989. Its programs and ministries, not only in the church but in the community, make "Old Abington Church" as much a force today as it was in its early years.

*Rounded Romanesque features blend easily and warmly
with the Gothic ceiling to create a space for reverence and worship.*

Abington Presbyterian Church

TOUR

Started as a log cabin church in the middle of a graveyard in 1714, Abington Presbyterian now encompasses several buildings that are linked with the church building itself. The complex includes the Christian Education Building, its most recent addition in 1957, as well as the Parish Hall, dedicated in 1927. The first holds classrooms, meeting rooms, and a social parlor while the latter is a large room used for dinners and large gatherings. On the lower level of this building are additional classrooms for Sunday School.

However, it is the stone church with its elongated spire rising high above the building situated on two of the oldest roads in the area, that dominates all attention. The present church was rebuilt in 1896 but generally follows the shape of the building that had preceded it. On October 6, 1895, fire devoured a major part of the church. The remnant of the bell that had originally hung in the tower was melted down, recast in miniature replicas, and sold to fund the rebuilding. John Wanamaker, who was so involved with the founding of sister church, Jenkintown's Grace Presbyterian, generously donated a new bell to ring forth on Sundays.

The doors that lead to the narthex, directly below this bell tower, hint at the event that destroyed the earlier church. In gold and the silver of palladium leaf, the Tree of Life spirals upward, symbolic of Christ's church that continues to grow. Above the tree is the phoenix, its brilliant purple wings spread to encompass the entire panel. Beneath the bird, the raging fire of its self-immolation burns. As the phoenix dies after a long life of three to five hundred years, a new bird rises from the funeral pyre. Beginning again the cycle of life, the phoenix continues through time to triumph over death. Out of the ashes of the early church then, Abington Presbyterian Church rose again, to rebuild

The gold and silver "Tree of Life" doors.

the sanctuary and to renew the church's vitality.

Through the narthex, past the glass screen containing etched illustrations of various psalms and into the nave, the visitor enters a church that is made of a mixture of two distinct architectural styles. The roof line of the church is immediately identifiable as the typical Gothic ceiling. However, the arches in this church are rounded, seen in the separation of nave and chancel and in the tops of the windows. Within the wooden wainscotting, the rounded arches are repeated, separated at intervals by fluted columns. The softening of the forms grows from the Romanesque tradition and, within this church, blends easily with the more Gothic influences.

The written word is important in this interior. Around the perimeter of the roof, passages from the Old and New Testaments instruct the worshipper. In the arch before the chancel, scrolls containing the words of Jesus as expressed in the Beatitudes stand out in black lettering against the white unfolded scrolls.

There are six stained glass windows in the nave, each of which contains three separate scenes. Along the south wall, Old Testament figures reach back to the church's spiritual beginnings. The window closest to the narthex in the south wall depicts the expulsion of Adam and Eve from the Garden of Eden in the lowest scene. Above, contained in its own medallion, is Abraham preparing to sacrifice Isaac, and at the top is Noah building the Ark. Above all these scenes is a small hand representing God's driving presence in each event. The next three windows portray other important figures: Joseph, Moses, King David, Elijah, and Amos. Also along this wall are marble plaques that honor the men who have served as the church's pastors.

The story of Jesus begins in the south transept with a large window that portrays the Nativity and the Baptism of Christ. Following this window, other scenes are depicted: the Annunciation, Christ's childhood, and in the Window of Triumph in the north transept, the Resurrection. Other elements of Christ's life are shown in successive windows.

In 1959 enlargements were made to the sanctuary and to the transept. Behind the rounded arches, additional seats were placed to accommodate the growing church family. Notice the simplicity of the columns themselves that serve as a solid base for the dividing partition. At the top of each column, four crosses covered in gold leaf continue the Christian symbolism.

It is the chancel, the focal point of the church, that dramatically dominates the church. The fifty-eight-rank Moller pipe organ, installed in 1969, is placed here. The walls are painted in a rich turquoise that is repeated in the carpeting. Against the west wall, the reredos rises high against the wall. Falling from the brass crown at the top of the reredos, is the white and gold dossal cloth, woven with the word PAX, for *"the peace that passeth understanding."* As in other churches the dossal, paraments and orphreys are changed as different colors reflect the events of the liturgical year.

Within the reredos, the intricately hand-carved cross hangs. The most powerful symbol of Christianity here is depicted with the growing vine representing Christianity as a growing force. On the cross the Greek letters Chi and Rho are etched, the oldest monogram used in reference to Christ. Finally, Christ's name is spelled in ancient Greek letters: XPICTOC.

Above on the chancel ceiling symbols of the Four Evangelists have been included, as well as the words of the angels on the first Christmas: *"Glory to God in the highest. On earth peace, good will toward men."* All these details lend to the beauty of this area of the church. But it is the large rose window, set deeply into the wall above the reredos, that captures all attention. In the center Christ holds a cross-topped globe to symbolize His worldwide inspiration. He ascends to heaven and is surrounded by angels. The radiating panels contain representations of *"The Seven Last Words of Christ from the Cross."*

What is unusual about the rose window is the detailed use of gold leaf which adds a richness and dimension not seen in many other church windows. The window gains power from the brilliantly colored glass and metal ribs that separate the pieces of glass. However, the figures within, the large depiction of Christ, are formed by the fashioning of gold-leafed metal, so that they do not merely exist within the world of the glass-maker's craft. Rather, the figures have more dimension, more weight than usually afforded by glass alone. The result is an interesting combination of metal and glass where the colors add to the already fashioned gold figures, enhancing what has come before.

Abington Presbyterian Church also houses a smaller, more intimate chapel. The two windows here focus on Presbyterian history in America and in Abington. The window to the right captures details of this church's long history. At the bottom is a portrait of William Jennings Bryant who spoke at the church on its two-hundreth anniversary. Above him is President Benjamin Harrison who, on the anniversary of the Log College, the forerunner of Princeton Univer-

One of two Chapel windows depicting history of the Church.

sity, joined John Wanamaker in festivities held here and visited historic graves. Next George Whitefield, evangelist, is remembered as he spoke to over 2000 in the Abington church yard. At the top is Malachi Jones, the first pastor of the church, a depiction of the first log church above him and the second church below. This is a small window that is nevertheless packed with details from the extensive history of the church.

History is something that can not be ignored when visiting Abington Presbyterian Church. The cemetery itself, first used in 1728, is the resting place for a wide range of people who were instrumental in the development of this area. The son and grandson of William Tennant, who founded Log College, are buried there. The bodies of six Revolutionary War veterans as well as the veterans of every war since then are found in the graveyard. There is the grave of Colonel Charles G. McCawley, Commandant of the United States Marines. To this day, a detachment of Marines comes yearly on the anniversary of the Corps to perform a ceremony at the grave. The founder of the first school in Hatboro, Robert Loller, is also

The Cemetery, dating from 1728.

buried in the grave yard. And the grave of Susan B. Smith, who founded the first Children's Missionary Society, the oldest in the United States, and who was an early advocate of women's rights, can be found here.

Abington Presbyterian Church works towards its future while always recalling its past. In a case in a central hallway are yellowed memorabilia of the church history. The church is proud of the years of continuous service to the community and to the faithful. The stories of the past circulate in all detail, recapturing slivers of history that belong to all who make their homes here. The cemetery testifies to the many people who once lived here when Abington was "country," the outlying areas around a growing city.

But, as the phoenix on the front doors reminds us, the importance of spiritual rebirth has not been ignored. The church is vibrant in its many programs as well as in its extensive history, evolving still to offer answers for today's world, and making faith one of the primary solutions.

Epilogue:
CHRISTIANS AND JEWS: A NEW AND A BETTER WORLD*

How shall we conclude our tour through the churches and synagogues of the Old York Road corridor? As we enter the final decade of the second Christian millenium, what do Christians have to say to Jews? and Jews to Christians?

Clearly, "how to relate to Jews" is not the primary concern of those Christians who attend and support the twelve churches described in these pages, nor is "how to relate to Christians" the primary concern of the Jews who are involved in the four synagogues. But the relationships of Jews to Christians and of Judaism and Christianity were very much on the mind of the editor of this volume and, in fact, inspired its publication.

If this book is to have any real impact on our Cheltenham-Jenkintown-Abington community, it must provide us with more than just a pleasant tour through the houses of worship of our neighbors. It must provide us with a basis for serious dialogue, dialogue that may work to break down stereotypes and deep-seated prejudices and transform us into a true community.

Thus, I pose these questions to the men and women of good will who frequent our churches and synagogues. How shall American Jews, half a century after the Holocaust, relate to Christianity in the new millenium? How shall we respond to the rapprochement that seems evident in the recent spate of Catholic and Protestant position papers on relations with Jews? And how respond to those anti-Semitic acts and words that seem to be almost reflexive for many Christians but that invoke in Jews hideous memories of Auschwitz?

The editor is the grandson of gentle and loving

*This essay, by Rabbi Simeon J. Maslin, appeared in Christian Century, March 7, 1990 in a revised version.

Jews who lived through Polish pogroms. They saw a son trampled under the hooves of horsemen whom they identified only as "Christians." They fled to America to escape what they saw as Christian persecution. Those same gentle grandparents who showered me with tender love taught me to cross the street and spit when passing a church. That generation of immigrant Jews met Christian hate with Jewish hate, Christian contempt with Jewish contempt. They had no other choices.

But what about my generation, the generation of American liberal Jews who feel increasingly alienated from old world Orthodoxy and increasingly wooed by Christian denominations that are inviting us to dialogue in the spirit of those position papers redefining Christian attitudes toward Jews? All of those Holocaust-inspired papers begin with the frank admission that for centuries the Church was guilty of teaching that Christianity had superceded Judaism, and that the result of that false doctrine was the fomenting of hatred and persecution. And they go on to explain that Christianity and Judaism are two legitimate paths to the one God and that any Christian who is guilty of anti-Semitism is guilty also of the denial of Christ.

Protestantism, of course, has many voices. And while most of the mainstream, liberal churches are coming to a new appreciation of their Jewish roots and condemning old anti-Semitic attitudes, there are still some strident, old Gospel Protestant voices that teach that it was the Jews who were guilty of the death of Christ and that anti-Semitic acts and attitudes are well deserved.

Pope John Paul II — the official voice of Catholicism — is hard to pin down. On the one hand, he refuses to recognize Israel; he has granted audiences to Yasir Arafat and Kurt Waldheim; he has called for

Israel to withdraw from Jerusalem; and, on a theological level, he has delivered homilies that teach that Christianity has superceded and replaced Judaism as God's partner in covenant. On the other hand, he has spoken poignantly about Jewish martyrdom while condemning Nazism; he has gone to the synagogue of Rome and declared that the Jews are the legitimate and honored older brothers of Catholics; on the twentieth anniversary of *Nostra Aetate* he declared that "anti-Semitism, in its ugly and sometimes violent manifestations, must be completely eradicated;" and, most recently, he indicated that he would like the Carmelite nuns to withdraw from that Auschwitz convent that has been a bone in the throat of Jews.

Let me be so bold as to suggest that, as we approach the twenty-first century, either Christians will have to concede that the Sinaitic covenant between God and Israel is an eternal covenant and that to teach or practice or even hint at anti-Semitism is to deny the teachings of Christ, or Christianity is doomed. If Christianity is to endure as an intellectual, moral and spiritual force into its third millennium, it can do so only arm-in-arm with Judaism. Why? Because wise and committed Christians are all too aware that the Holocaust raised agonizing questions about the validity of Christianity.

As for those on the Jewish side: we must learn to accept the fact that we are living in a Christian country. As much as we might fight against prayers in public schools, against creches on city property, and against political leaders who would have the nerve to state openly that this is a Christian country, facts are facts. Jews constitute only two-and-a-half percent of the American polity. And while that other ninety-seven-and-a-half percent may not all be confessing Christians — many are secularists, humanists and out-right pagans — it is Christianity which defines the religious climate of America.

American Jews must be aware of what is being taught and what is being practiced in Christian churches, not in order to emulate Christians and certainly not in order to convert them, but quite simply because, as I said, it is Christianity which defines religion in America. If Jews want the Jewish message to be heard and understood here in America, if Jews want to participate in the free marketplace of ideas, if we take seriously the sacred Jewish mission

"to be a light to the nations," then the Jewish message must be clothed in a vocabulary comprehensible to Christians. That is one of the realities of an America on the threshold of the third Christian millennium. And I, for one, find it a stimulating and a challenging reality. Thus this book, designed to promote dialogue in our area.

Given this overwhelmingly Christian environment, then, what options are available to Jews? One choice is to turn inward, to turn our backs on Christianity, recalling the inquisitions and the pogroms and the crusades and the cross-burnings and the fomenting of anti-Semitism that were a part of Christianity from the days of the early Church Fathers through the Holocaust. We can opt to go it alone, and Orthodox Jews have clearly made that choice. They are more and more becoming a separatist elite and retreating to ethnic enclaves in a few big cities.

The other choice? No, it is not to forgive and forget. Jews were never taught to turn the other cheek. The other choice is to work honestly and lovingly with that growing body of righteous Christians who look to Judaism as to an older sibling, who are seeking to expiate Christian guilt for the Holocaust, and who recognize that Christianity and Judaism need each other desperately if religion in twenty-first-century America is to offer a compelling alternative to unbridled consumerism, to the popular philosophy of Me! Me! Me!, and to arid secularism.

There were two very important words in that last sentence: *honestly* and *lovingly*. Let me expand a bit on those two essential adverbs. First, honestly.

One of the real problems in interfaith relations is politeness, the fear of offending. I am absolutely convinced that the majority of well-meaning Christians do not understand why it is that Jews were so upset at the idea of a Christian convent dedicated to prayer for the souls of all those who died in Auschwitz. Certainly Cardinal Glemp, the Primate of Poland, did not understand why it was inappropriate for an order of Christian nuns to be praying there, in the shadow of a twenty-three foot cross, for the souls of Jews. His sudden reversal was the result of political pressure, not of having seen the light.

Yes, I know that non-Jews perished in Auschwitz as well. But Auschwitz is for Jews a synonym for the Holocaust. A third or more of the Jews who perished at the hands of the Nazis perished in that one place, Auschwitz. Auschwitz *is* the Holocaust for Jews.

And so we must ask Cardinal Glemp and all those well-meaning Christians who did not understand the objection to a Christian convent in Auschwitz, honestly and pointedly: "Do you believe that those millions of innocent Jews who died so cruelly in Auschwitz would want a Christian house of worship to mark the place of their martyrdom? their Passion?"

We must remind Christians that those murdered Jews could hear the joyous pealing of church bells from towns around Auschwitz and Birkenau every Sunday morning. The good Christians who prayed in those churches in 1943 and '44 were not praying then for the souls of Jews. Would those murdered innocents want the Carmelite nuns to pray for them now?

Dear Christian friends, if we are to work together for the salvation of our world, then we must address each other honestly. And so I must explain to Christians why Jews of my grandfather's generation spat when they passed churches. I must explain why it is an affront to the sacred memories of six million Jews to allow a Christian shrine to mark their charnel house.

You see: *one hundred Christs crucified on crosses from Calvary to Cracow to that Carmelite convent could not begin to atone for the cruel and coldly calculated criminal acts committed by people raised as Christians against my people.* You can give the excuse that I hear from many of my Christian colleagues: that the killers were really pagans. You can say in all truth that their acts were a denial of Christian doctrine. But the fact is that almost all of them were raised as Christians and that most of them thought of themselves as Christians. We must face that fact honestly.

The second essential adverb that I mentioned a few moments ago was lovingly. How, in Heaven's name, having said what I just said about Christians, can I say that we must work with righteous Christians lovingly? Am I, perhaps, being patronizing? or even hypocritical? No, not at all.

I have come to understand that with all the tragic Christian-Jewish conflict that has darkened the history of Western Civilization and shrouded the presence of God — with it all, my faith and my hopes for the future of our civilization are closer to those of liberal Christians than they are to the Chassidim of Brooklyn and the black-hatted zealots of Jerusalem. It

does not please me to say that, and I wish that it were not true, but it is. And the obverse truth is that the superstition, the obscurantism, the self-righteousness and the blind fanaticism of ultra-Orthodoxy are more in tune with born-again, Bible-thumping, charismatic Christianity and with Shiite Muslim fundamentalism than they are with American liberal Judaism.

Religious liberals — Christians and Jews — need partners in a world that is increasingly hostile to rationality, morality and freedom of conscience. We need partners who share our deep concerns about homelessness and hunger, about the toxicity of our environment, about racism and about basic human rights. We need partners who believe that governments should be more concerned about the care of the aged and indigent than about the care of fertilized ova, flags, and nuclear stockpiles. We Jews hope to find such partners in the ranks of those people whom the ancient rabbis called Righteous Gentiles.

Some of our readers may have visited the Yad Va-Shem Holocaust Memorial Museum in Jerusalem. As you pass through its halls, weeping at the pictures of murdered innocents and the artifacts of the most technologically efficient murder industry in the history of inhumanity, you can feel your heart filling with hatred, hatred of *them.* I once actually heard a man, standing at the exit of that dark hall that houses the eternal flame, sobbing: "I wish God would send down a fire on all of them."

But then, as you proceed from the museum to your bus or car, you walk down a tree-shaded lane that is called "The Path of the Righteous Gentiles." At the base of each tree there is a little plaque with a name and a country. All the names are of Christians who risked their lives in order to save the lives of Jews. There are hundreds of such trees, each with its honored Christian name. One might wish that there were thousands, but there are hundreds. Every one of them was a Christian hero.

We Jews must seek out the Righteous Christians among us here in America with love. I feel certain that there are thousands of them, ready and waiting to enter into dialogue. They need us, and we need them. We need each other, not so that we might blend into a simple-minded Abie's Irish Rose Jewish-Christian mish-mash. No, to the contrary. We need each other for the kind of dialogue that can stimulate, enrich and deepen our respective faiths. We need each other to prove to the world that, with honesty and love, two great and separate traditions can work together to fashion a nobler society.

It was with love that I read the words of Bernard Cardinal Law of Boston, addressed to the Carmelite Sisters at Auschwitz.* He began his Open Letter to them by telling of his life-long admiration for their contemplative vocation. And then he went on to describe a pilgrimage that he had made to Auschwitz a few years ago in a group of Catholics and Jews. He wrote:

> … We walked in numbed silence through this monument to inhumanity, to sin in all its horror. The barbaric cruelty was made poignantly present by the survivors in our midst. We gathered at the memorial wall, Jews and Catholics, and raised our hearts and voices in prayerful remembrance of all who had died, … Our prayer concluded as, through our tears, we greeted one another with "Shalom."

Cardinal Law went on to plead with the Carmelite sisters "to go the extra mile," to withdraw willingly from Auschwitz for the sake of reconciliation.

> … In a world so painfully divided between rich and poor, black and white, Moslem, Christian and Jew, that sign of reconciling love which is within your power could have a meaning far greater than the immediate context of controversy. It could [give] substance to the cry of all civilized people, "Never again."

I pray that I am not being naive as I admit that I resonate to the words of a prince of the church that for so many centuries despised and persecuted our people. I will go further. I feel a greater spiritual kinship with Cardinal Law and with many other righteous Christians than I do with those Jews who are more concerned with the minute details of the dietary laws and strict Sabbath observance than they are with their daily ethical conduct and human rights.

Please do not misunderstand my words. Thank God, there are many, many Jews who are deeply concerned about ethics and human rights. Obviously, my own people will always be closest to my heart, because I can share with them both my universal human concerns and my parochial Jewish concerns. But my heart is warm enough to radiate love to people of any religion, any nationality or any color who live and work for the benefit of the human race. I return to the letter from Cardinal Law:

> … How necessary it is for men and women of differing faiths and backgrounds to meet one another in mutual respect and love. How necessary it is for us to share our personal and collective memories, and to allow the balm of genuine, mutual love to heal the wounds that for too long have divided us.

Cardinal Law's voice is surely not a lonely one in Christian circles today.

The world of religion has changed in the brief generation of my rabbinate. O, I know that anti-Semitism still exists, as surely as I know that there are still Jews who curse and spit when they pass churches. But it is there precisely that our choice lies.

Shall we join the ranks of those — Jews and Christians — who live only in the past, whose hearts are governed by hate, and who live for dominance and revenge? Or shall we join the ranks of those — Jews and Christians — whose lives are dedicated to the fashioning of a new and a better world, a world firmly rooted in the rich soil of diverse traditions but joyously open to the possibility of *"Love thy neighbor as thyself?"*

I have made my choice. I hear my sacred Torah calling to me from Sinai: *"Choose Life!"* I choose a world where brothers and sisters wipe away each others' tears and greet one another with "Shalom."

The Pilot (Boston), 8/30/89.

Glossary

This Glossary is divided into two parts. In Part I the religions and demoninations represented by the sixteen churches and synagogues described in this book are very briefly identified. In Part II ritual, historic, foreign and architectural terms found in the text are defined.

PART I

BAPTIST   A Protestant denomination, founded early in the seventeenth century in opposition to infant baptism and in favor of strict separation of church and state. The primary authority among Baptists is the Bible, and true believers accept Christ as their personal savior. There is no governing creedal statement, and churches are autonomous.

CHRISTIAN SCIENCE   Founded by Mary Baker Eddy in Boston in 1879. Her original intention was not to found a separate denomination but to influence churches to accept her system of divine healing through faith. Local churches throughout the world are branches of the "Mother Church," the First Church of Christ, Scientist, in Boston, and all adhere to Mrs. Eddy's interpretations of Bible.

EPISCOPALIAN   A Protestant denomination, established by the separation of King Henry VIII from the authority of Rome in 1534. Episcopalian authority is the Bible as interpreted by traditions and the triennial convention of bishops, priests and laypeople. The Apostles' Creed is basic, but Episcopalian churches range from liberal to the acceptance of most Roman Catholic dogma.

GREEK ORTHODOX   The Orthodox churches (Greek and Russian) trace their origins to first-century Christian proselytizing. After centuries of doctrinal disputes with Rome, the Orthodox churches broke away in 1054. Authority stems from the Bible as interpreted by the first seven church councils (up to Nicaea II in 787). Bishops govern in council. Church doctrine emphasizes the Resurrection rather than the Crucifixion.

JEWISH   The earliest of the three great western monotheistic religions (Judaism, Christianity, Islam), based on the law of Moses and the later interpretations of rabbinic tradition. Synagogues are autonomous and are governed by boards of members with the counsel of their rabbis. Weekly Sabbath services take place on Friday evenings and Saturdays rather than Sunday.

LUTHERAN   A Protestant denomination, established by Martin Luther through his secession from the authority of Rome in 1517. Lutheran authority is in the Bible as spelled out in the Augsburg Confession (1530) and later creeds. Lutherans believe in salvation by faith alone, through divine grace. There is a considerable theological range between liberals and fundamentalists.

METHODIST   A Protestant denomination, established by Dr. John Wesley from within the Church of England (Episcopalian) in 1738. Methodist authority is in the Bible, as interpreted by tradition and reason;

administrative authority is vested in annual conferences and bishops. Theology is similar to Episcopalian.

PRESBYTERIAN　A Protestant denomination, which evolved from the Calvinist Reformation during the sixteenth century. John Knox founded the Scotch Presbyterian Church in 1560. Authority is in the Bible and a highly structured system of representative ministers and laypersons (presbyters). Doctrine emphasizes the sovereignty and justice of God.

QUAKERS　See Society of Friends.

ROMAN CATHOLIC　Tradition traces the origin of the Catholic (universal) church to Jesus' selection of St. Peter as the first vicar of the church. The Pope (Bishop of Rome) has authority in all matters of faith, morals and the interpretation of tradition. Salvation is achieved through faith and a system of elaborate sacraments. As the result of recent Vatican Councils, Roman Catholicism has gone through a period of rapid change.

SOCIETY OF FRIENDS　A Christian group, commonly called Quakers, founded in England in the seventeenth century by George Fox. Friends believe that God's grace is freely given to all people and that all have the Light of Christ. The Bible is accepted as inspired by God but is subordinate to interpretation in the light of God's spirit. Pacifism is one of the fundamentals of the Society of Friends. Pennsylvania was founded by a member of the Society, William Penn, as a "holy experiment."

UKRAINIAN CATHOLIC　An ethnic sub-division of the Roman Catholic Church, involving people from the Ukrainian region of the Soviet Union.

PART II

ANNUNCIATION　The Christian belief that in Jesus Christ God "has visited and redeemed His people" (Luke 1:68). This news was announced, hence "the Annunciation," to Mary by the angel Gabriel.

ANTHROPOMORPHIC　The description of God, using a vocabulary of human features or characteristics.

ANTIMENSION　In the Eastern churches, a consecrated cloth containing relics and kept on the altar.

ARK　The closet, generally situated in the center of the eastern wall of American synagogues, in which is kept the scrolls of the Torah.

APSE　A projecting part of a church building, often semi-circular and vaulted, behind the altar, often the place where the choir is located.

AUSCHWITZ　During the Holocaust, the Nazi concentration camp in Poland where the largest number of Jews were killed.

BANYA　In Ukrainian churches, the onion-shaped cupolas that often rise above the roof like spires.

BAPTISM　The ceremony of proclaiming one a Christian with the use of water, by immersion, pouring over or sprinkling.

BEATITUDES　The verses in the Sermon on the Mount (Matthew 5:3-12) that begin: "Blessed are …".

BEMA　(Related to *Bima* below) The part of an Eastern church that contains the altar.

BIMA　The raised platform at the front of a synagogue from which the service is conducted.

BYZANTINE   Related to the Eastern rite of the Christian church, deriving from Constantinople (formerly Byzantium, contemporary Istanbul).

CANTOR   The officient who chants the service in a synagogue; called in Hebrew *Chazzan* or *Hazzan*.

CATECHISM   Instruction in the doctrines of a Christian church, usually a set of prescribed questions and answers.

CHASSIDIM   Lit., pious ones. The ultra-Orthodox Jewish sect that clings to many of the customs and mystical beliefs of seventeenth-century Poland.

CHANCEL   The part of a church in which are located the altar or communion table, the lectern and the pulpit.

CHAZZAN   See Cantor.

CHERUBIM   Celestial beings, usually with wings and human heads, akin to angels, often depicted as guardians of sacred places or messengers of God.

CLERESTORY   An outside wall of a building (usually a church) which rises above an adjoining roof and is pierced by windows, admitting light to the interior.

COMMUNION   A celebration of the Lord's Supper or Eucharist in which the communicant receives the elements of the Eucharist.

CONSERVATIVE   One of the three main branches of American Judaism (along with Orthodox and Reform). The Conservative branch adheres to traditional Judaism but is more moderate and progressive than the Orthodox.

DEACON   In Roman Catholicism, a cleric below the rank of priest. In several Protestant churches, either a candidate for ordination or a lay leader involved in the governance of the church.

DIACONICON   In the Eastern churches, the sacristy at the right or north side of the Bema.

DOSSAL   An ornamental cloth hung above and behind the altar.

ECCLESIASTICAL   Related to the church as a formal institution.

EUCHARIST   A central rite in many Christian churches in which bread and wine are consecrated, given by the clergy to the congregation, and consumed as symbols of union with the body and blood of Christ.

EVANGELIST   An author of one of the four Gospels or a person who seeks to convert people to Christianity by preaching the Gospel.

GOSPEL   The story (or good news) about the life of Jesus, recorded in the first four books of the New Testament.

GOTHIC   Relating to the civilization of the Goths; often used to describe the style of church architecture developed in Western Europe between the twelfth and sixteenth centuries, in which pointed arches and vaults replaced the roundness of the Romanesque.

HAZZAN   See Cantor.

HIERARCH   A religious leader of high office.

ICON   Usually in Eastern churches, a sacred image depicting Christ, Mary, a saint or religious story.

ICONOSTASIS   In Eastern churches, a screen or partition decorated with icons and separating the Bema from the Nave.

INCARNATION   The union of the divine with the human, in the person of Jesus Christ.

JUSTINIAN   Relating to the Byzantine emperor Justinian (sixth century), under whom Eastern church influences spread to the West.

KETUBAH   The marriage document or contract, often quite ornate, used in Jewish wedding ceremonies.

KOSHER   Actually *Kasher*, meaning acceptable, fit to be used or eaten in accordance with Jewish ritual or dietary laws.

LITURGY   The language and ritual of a religious service.

MENORAH   Usually a seven-branched candelabrum as in the Mosaic Tabernacle or the ancient Temple of Jerusalem. (The Chanukah Menorah has eight branches, plus a servant candle, representing the eight days of the Maccabean miracle.)

METROPOLITAN   The head of a province of the Eastern church who has his headquarters in a large city.

MINYAN   The Jewish prayer quorum of ten people (the Orthodox require males) above the age of thirteen needed to conduct congregational worship.

MITZVAH   Hebrew word for a divine commandment. A Bar (m.)/Bat (f.) Mitzvah is a ceremony in which a young person accepts adult responsibility for the performance of commandments.

NARTHEX   A vestibule or porch leading into the church.

NATIVITY   The birth of Jesus Christ.

NAVE   The long central hall or the main part of a church.

NER TAMID   The eternal light which usually hangs above and in front of the Ark in synagogues.

NOSTRA AETATE   The Declaration of the Roman Catholic Church on attitudes toward Jews, inspired by Pope John XXIII and the Second Vatican Council. The Declaration, recognizing the validity of Judaism, was promulgated by Pope Paul VI in 1965.

ONEG SHABBAT   Lit., the joy of the Sabbath, based on Isaiah (58:13). In the modern synagogue, this is the usual name for the social hour following a Sabbath service.

ORDINARY   A prelate who exercises jurisdiction over a specified territorial area of the church.

ORPHREY   The ornamental, often embroidered, border of an ecclesiastical vestment.

ORTHODOX   One of the three main branches of American Judaism (along with Conservative and Reform). The Orthodox branch accepts the binding authority of ancient Jewish law as the word of God.

PALLADIAN   A revived classic style of architecture based on the work of Palladio (sixteenth century), often used to refer to a central window crowned with an arch.

PARAMENTS   Ornamental ecclesiastical hangings or garments.

PENDENTIVE   A triangular, supporting architectural feature, usually above a column of a rectangular room, used to support a dome.

PENTECOST   A Christian festival on the seventh Sunday after Easter, commemorating the descent of the Holy Spirit on the Apostles. Also used in Judaism as a translation of the Shavuot festival, seven weeks after Passover.

POGROM   An organized massacre of a defenseless minority, often used to describe anti-Semitic riots in Eastern Europe.

PROSKOMEDIA   In the Eastern churches, the table in the Sanctuary where the Eucharist is prepared.

RECTORY   A rector's residence or a church parsonage.

REFORM   One of the three main branches of American Judaism (along with Conservative and Orthodox). The Reform branch adheres only to those traditions that can be meaningful to modern Jews.

REREDOS   An ornamental screen or partition, located behind an altar.

RESURRECTION   The rising of a person from the dead, especially the rising of Jesus Christ after the Crucifixion.

RIPIDIA   The rays emanating like starbursts from icons, used in sacred processions.